A Leopard Can't Change Its Spots

And Other Lies We're Told

Robin P. Currie

ARCHWAY
PUBLISHING

Archway Publishing books may be ordered through booksellers or by contacting:

Archway Publishing
1663 Liberty Drive
Bloomington, IN 47403
www.archwaypublishing.com
1 (888) 242-5904

Interior images by Gordon Johnson.

Scripture taken from the King James Version of the Bible.

ISBN: 978-1-4808-8029-0 (sc)
ISBN: 978-1-4808-8030-6 (hc)
ISBN: 978-1-4808-8028-3 (e)

Library of Congress Control Number: 2019910497

Print information available on the last page.

Archway Publishing rev. date: 08/26/2019

For my mother and grandmother.

"But refuse profane and old wives fables, and exercise thyself rather unto godliness".
(1 Timothy 4:7 KJVA).

I discern.

Contents

Introduction

We've been duped, tricked, and fooled. Who did this? And why?

Blame the politicians--their reputations most certainly paint them as a dishonest bunch.

Parents have had a hand in it as well. But we love them, and we understand they were doing the best they could. And we acknowledge that all parents make mistakes even under the best of circumstances.

Shall we add school teachers to this list? Thousands of textbooks throughout the American public school system have been found to be incomplete, or even flat out wrong. Regardless, teachers are still compelled to teach certain things even with full awareness of error.

Media and marketing specialists are masters of manipulation. They often play upon lies. Subliminal marketing is a pervasive form of manipulation, which actually leads us to *think* we want or need something.

And here's a segment you've been waiting for me to mention--religious groups. Religious beginnings remind us of a history of love, devotion to God, and a desire to teach the goodness of our Creator. Please let us remember that religion is a methodology to seek God. It remains a vehicle for enlightenment for billions of people. But the ambiguity of the Holy Books, and human ego drives have made religions, for some, an agency of confusion, pain, and death. Thus, we have seen religious control and deception-- from the Crusades to early American Puritanism; from the Branch Davidians to Jonestown, Guyana. Yes, organized religion has collectively become a source of limiting beliefs, unhealthy conditioning, secret crimes, mind control, and war. And, sadly, today's humanity is forever left with a tragic and terrifying memory which now accompanies the phrase: "don't drink the Kool Aid".

This book is not intended to enter such a heavy and emotionally charged foray as was just described, but it bore mentioning. Instead, let us take a tongue in cheek approach as we suss out stupid sayings. Come laugh with me as we realize ridiculous deceptions and hilarious lies that are heard and said constantly. Most importantly, let us roll our eyes together and find humor in the irony of our own beliefs that have served to limit us.

And finally, the last group of liars--you and me! Yes, I mean you. And when we point one finger at someone, three are pointing back at us, so, yes, I mean me! We deceive when we pass on debilitating and toxic teachings which have no basis in reality. Those beliefs are merely distortions--we have not done our homework. Do our negative manipulations continue to perpetuate generation upon generation of self-fulfilling prophecy? Are we reaping what we sow? Consider the Hebrew hymn: "sow in tears, reap in joy". Can we alter the illusion, and convert our seeds to purity, abundance, love, compassion, and truth? Then we can watch them grow. Let us start here, and now.

Thus is necessitated the discussion of limiting beliefs. The purpose of this book is to dispel and refute lifetimes of limiting beliefs which are imposed upon all of us. But now I ask: is the concept of limiting beliefs actually true? Are they real? Is this quite possibly the greatest deception of all? Are we *told* we have limiting beliefs, when in fact we have none? In one of the chapters within this book, you will see my dissection of the distortion **"we're only human"**, which gives credence to a dirty little lie about humans being flawed. The simple assembly of the two words, *limiting* and *beliefs*, is possibly meant to serve us--to awaken us to the awareness of the myriad of manipulations we face as humans. Or, instead, is it a profound untruth which, when believed, places upon us weaknesses and acceptance of a predestined measure of suffering, thus making the words "limiting beliefs" the evilest of all deceptions?

Oh, the irony of the message within the story *The Adventures of Pinocchio*, by Carlo Collodi (1826-1890). Collodi was a political satirist, a novelist, and a journalist. This particular piece of his has become a world-renowned favorite among parents. Adults everywhere present this work to their children and teach them that lies are obvious. Pinocchio's mishaps tell children that all would-be deceptions are written all over their adorable little faces. And oftentimes they are.

But let us take the view from the top: can we not see, camouflaged within the story, one of humanity's greatest acts of fraud? This tale was fashioned by a humorist. Yet with a serious air, it is quite sternly used to conceal the real manipulation. What is referred to as "the moral of the story" within Collodi's masterpiece is indeed a lesson we do not ever learn. I wonder how many youngsters watch the movie and laugh--seeing the entire story as a great, big joke. And, at the same time I wonder how many naive and pure little souls take it to heart and make inward vows to never fib. How funny that these same innocents likely believe that others have understood this principle as well. Thus, for these little ones, the lesson itself is a fable. Our noses do not grow longer with each falsehood. And indeed, we live amongst great deceptions, and hidden deceptions, in a society enraptured by success, money, and power.

In the story, Pinocchio experiences the devastating effects of his own lies. This represents another immense and cruel irony. We discover that the true tragedy lies within the understanding that misrepresentations spoken to us are, truly, equally nefarious to the lies we speak to others. As a collective, do we continue to exert massive control over each other for the purpose of attaining our own desires? Do we cruise through life as programmed individuals, not looking into the deep waters of what is right for us? Are we asleep? How do we awaken? When do we, as a collective, seek and find truth? Look between the layers--read between the lines and see that true power is found through love, compassion, the mastery of self, and, above all, truth.

My father embodies what the Irish call a seanchai, a master storyteller, and he has a few favorite movie scenes he loves to recant. One such is within the comedic film *Sunshine Cleaning*. The family in this movie is quite farcical. The dad is questioned by one of his adult children as he intentionally paints a marketing slogan (which happens to be a dishonest one) on the outside of their vehicle. The dad's response: "It's a business lie. It's different from a life lie". That says it all. And this situation brings to mind that lies have colors. Yes, some are white, and some are not. So therefore, since white somehow represents purity, then that suggests that white lies are okay. You know, they're sort of like business lies.

Ah, the beloved childhood game of "Telephone". Another amusing irony, and a foggy demonstration of not what *might* happen, but what *has* happened. An original, secret message from the first player is passed along from one person to the next. By the time the message reaches the end of the phone chain and is announced by the final receiver, it has most often hilariously twisted into an entirely different message! The cruel joke here is that we cleverly use this game to demonstrate that which *has occurred* within our society. The goal is awareness and the players intend to prevent distortion of the communication. The warning is to seek clarity, and to not believe everything that we hear. Ha!

And, as is customary for me, I refer to Holy Scripture. I do not cite bible references to prove my point, or to dissuade you from your own beliefs. Some say the Christian bible is the Book of Truth, and others say it is a pack of lies. For me it is a code, and a mystery to be unraveled. For within the ambiguous musings and creative expressions of the mind, put forth by humans through many ages of spiritual evolution, I find my questions. These mysteries have guided me through my spiritual journey since the age of six and continue to do so each day. You will see scripture sprinkled throughout these pages but let me present to you the very foundation of my intent in writing this book: the book of John speaks of truth in a profound and fascinating way.

"If we say that we have fellowship with him, and walk in darkness, we lie, and do not the truth." (1 John 1:6 KJVA). Saint John's verse says we "do not" the truth. It does not speak of telling the truth, it speaks of truth as an action--as something we do! This realization, for me, served as a catalyst to search for truth everywhere, and in everything I do.

Another interesting and unwitting contributor to this work is John Lyly (1553-1606), a contemporary of William Shakespeare. From within Lyly's comedic and, obviously, quite enduring work we find the origins of many phrases commonly employed today. A few of them are cited within these pages, including Mr. Lyly's reference which he presumably admired from the Holy Bible. Herein is the source (Mr. Lyly's quote), from which I directly corroborate the comedy: "That euery thing will dispose it selfe according to Nature? Can the Aethiope change or alter his skinne? or the Leoparde his hewe?"

But how these teachings have changed! As years have rolled on, the satirical words of John Lyly have become pearls of wisdom! Perhaps this represents his grandest joke of all, and John Lyly is quite possibly looking down upon us in amusement and with immense satisfaction--mission accomplished! And it is quite notable to me that I was compelled to lean heavily upon the brilliant works of two men named John: Saint John of Patmos, and John Lyly. Coincidence?

As you continue your journey through this book, you will see sequences of words presented in **bold type**. Heads up! True, or not true? The presumed untruths are formatted differently than other text, but not dramatically so. You see--lies are sneaky. Thus, the formatting is subtle, to demonstrate the subtlety of the euphemism to which I refer. Deceptions are often so cleverly masked, we often discover that we have been completely blind to them. Additionally, the word strings in bold are meant to trigger moments of critical analysis for you, my dear reader. Once observed, the boldness of lies become clear. Only then, can one begin to wash clean and transmute the anxiety caused by deception.

A Leopard Can't Change Its Spots is created with the spirit of all things blue--the symbolic color of the throat chakra. The power of this energy system communicates only Truth. What, then, is Truth? It is different for each of us. But Truth surrounds us, hidden in plain sight, as a single, breathtakingly beautiful rose among the many thorns. It must it be sought, discovered, uncovered, and learned. The shroud must be removed from our eyes--the veil lifted. Then, and only then, is Truth manifested. And, through alchemy, the sacred flame of our own gnosis transforms the lies, the dross falls away, and only Truth remains.

The spirit of the leopard has remained with me throughout this project. From my perspective, this animal represents speed, strength, endurance, beauty, and power. He does not question his worth. To me, the leopard became representative of the truth I seek, the notion of new perspective, and the freedom of change. He was present, by my side, from the beginning. And now, my dream is that we all realize the truth of who we are. Let the Inner Child merge with the Sage, as we each discern truth from illusion. My prayer is for peace, which can be achieved through this process. My vision is as that of Saint John of Revelation: "The wolf will live with the lamb, the leopard will lie down with the goat, the calf and the lion and the yearling together; and a little child will lead them." (Isaiah 11:6 NIV).

PART ONE

THE BATTLEFIELD

For the past couple of years, I have been conducting an unofficial survey, using a single question. To each unsuspecting victim I ask: "Do you believe there is a time for war?" The results--I'll tell you later.

As you read the associated falsehoods within this section, you will see the vastly differing personalities between those who strive for peace, and those who pursue a different purpose. To demonstrate my point, I cite military leaders here--not so as to judge their character, rather to list people who appear, at least to me, comfortable with the concept of war: Napoleon Bonaparte, Winston Churchill, Joshua, Adolf Hitler, and Pope Urban. And next I refer to peacemakers and proponents of non-violence such as Mahatma Gandhi, Saint Stephen, Leo Tolstoy, and Martin Luther King, Jr.

Not to be forgotten are the ones in between, caught within the predicament of being on the fence--notably Arjuna, of the *Bhagavad Gita*. A similar ambivalence and range of viewpoints on war is also present within the Holy Bible. In the New Testament, Jesus incarnates to teach of love as the force of supreme power, and the true intent of

God. Yet we see, in the book of Joshua especially, a call to arms--the directing general: God, Himself. Also within the Old Testament, we find the book of Judges. The writings in Judges are all about conflict. They are quite gruesome, I might add. Many incidents chronicled in Judges present as snapshots of man's propensity to war.

Let's see what we have here: Jephthah burned his own daughter as an offering to God, Samson's eyes were gouged out by the Philistines, and then there's Judges 19. I've never been able to fully get my head around that story: someone chopped up a woman, quite symbolically, and that action became a catalyst for more war. Were the tribes of Israel just exploring how far their atrocities could go?

Here's what really puzzles me: who was the Levite of Judges 19? He wasn't important enough to even name. Did anyone even remember his name? Was he that insignificant? Yet, somehow, this unknown, unnamed man had enough influence to start a war. The hypocrisy is glaring here--as if anyone even cared about "the concubine". I mean, do you even know what they did to her? Yet the defense of her honor now became an excuse to fight. Perhaps I don't quite get it. Actually, I'm sure I don't quite get it. But who really gets war? Can anyone really understand it?

What, really, do we fight for: land, resources, power, judgement against each other, iron, revenge, religion, access to water? The list is endless. But what I do know is this: war and peace do not come from the same place. That, Friend, has become the overarching driver for the assembly of these pages--the distinction between what is real, and what is not.

War is no joke, and perhaps it does not belong in a book intended to be satirical. Yet, war itself presents as quite a study in lies, paradox, deception, and nefarious intent. Does it really matter if you are on the side of the "goodies", or of the "baddies"? Herein lies the absurdity--each side considers itself right. And I may be stepping into a minefield here, so I must express my highest respect for soldiers who have fought for my country, for the safety and security of all of us, and most importantly, for freedom to be won for others who are otherwise oppressed. There is nothing that compares with sacrifice of self for others, and for that all gratitude is due.

Yet how does one take a position against war while still claiming admiration for those who fight because they find purpose within the action? Or, how does one support war, with full knowledge of the suffering it will bestow upon innocents? Both questions continue to demonstrate complexity and contradiction. Such is the nature of war consciousness.

Am I providing clarity, or confusion? Understanding, or quagmire? Do I have the answers? Apologetically I say: no answers, only more questions. However, in the words of the charismatic Richard Dawson, "survey says": **Yes**.

Chapter 1

All's Fair in Love and War

This book is meant to be entertaining. However, given the seriousness of the elements here--Love and War, I take an air of respect. But what is actually meant by the ridiculousness of "**all's fair in love and war**"? I fear it is this: once war is declared, ethics no longer apply. The tenets of compassion, morality, and even basic humanity are off the table. Thus, we learn that there is no limit to how far each side will go in order to claim the victory. We also learn that all methods, regardless of how inhuman they may be, are acceptable. Even under international law and treaty, a measure of torture is acceptable, thus considered fair.

In the game of love, the same rule applies. We see obsessions galore, many depicted on the big screen. We see stories on the news, quite frequently, about stalking behavior. We perk our ears for the Monday morning recap of recent social dramas. We cannot wait to spread the news when someone in our social group has exacted revenge on a lover for a wrong. And how often I have heard encouragement for one to undermine relationships of others, if such relationship contains an object of your affection. We not only accept these activities, we thrive on them. Keying cars, slashing tires, and other forms of rage are exciting, and the gossip is exquisite. In the game of love, it is suddenly okay to do whatever is necessary to win. And isn't in interesting that cheating in a game is explicitly wrong, and specifically labelled as unfair. But where love is concerned, all bets are off.

The **all's fair in love and war** attitude is sometimes is quite visible within cultural groups and even court systems. Sometimes judges hand down more lenient sentences for murder and other violent crimes if the offense qualifies as a "crime of passion". This category especially applies to love triangles. If one discovers that a partner is cheating, there's a little bit of a grey area as to whether it's okay to kill. So now enters the excuse of provocation. Domestic killings can, and often do, continue to fall into the provocation loophole. Many courts are turning away from provocation as a mitigating circumstance, but in some societies it still matters. Thus, love actually becomes an excuse for violence, or even homicide. And many cultures still approve spousal correction (you know, for bad wives) and "honor killings". I'm not going to go any further with this one.

In no place do we see a more powerful paradox of the devastating human position--balancing the concepts of love and war--than in *The Bhagavad Gita*. This entire, spectacular piece is written on the battlefield. We directly empathize with the tragic position Arjuna finds himself in. He is most decidedly, and inextricably, torn between the two polarities of love and war. The outcomes of his decision are squarely in his hands--life or death. One must read "*The Gita*" and imagine Arjuna as each of us. He demonstrates the circuitous nature of war, and the oftentimes perceived impossibility that love can be the answer.

Arjuna must fight for those he loves. He is expected to honor his comrades and his kingdom. He is expected to protect his people. Sadly, Arjuna has loved ones in the ranks of the opposing army, and he is expected to kill them. He clings to the belief that war is never justified, and he clings to love--even the love for his enemies. In the eyes of this reluctant warrior, none of this is fair. To Arjuna, there are no spoils, only death and destruction.

Ah, yes, the "spoils". These represent the benefits of war and are awarded to the victor. Spoils can consist of anything, and everything.

First, we imagine seizure of property, money, valuable assets (art, jewels), and even people. Less tangible: power. But when we refer to spoils, do we go back to an original definition? Spoil, as a verb, actually meant to strip the skin off a dead animal. Gross. As a city girl, I didn't really need to know that. But it is notable, at least to me, that we continue to use that word. And it has morphed into a noun which is nearly synonymous with "prize".

We seek true love, but can there ever be true war? Makes no sense, does it? We would never speak of the spoils of love, would we? But think again. Is love not often equated with a quest, which, some hope, will result in conquest? But that's not love, you say! I agree. But love, and the pursuit of it, can indeed present as a battle. This is especially true in cases of suffering souls, like the character of Annie Wilkes in Stephen King's brilliant thriller, *Misery*. In this story, there seems to be no end to the measures this character will take to be with the man she loves. Her atrocities mount as she realizes the possibility that the love is unrequited. Still, in the throes of her passion, Annie determines that her actions are fair. Now, justification has redeemed her crimes.

My response to love and war as comparable elements: time for scripture. "Can the fig tree, my brethren, bear olive berries? either a vine, figs? so can no fountain both yield salt water and fresh". (James 3:12 KJVA). This, to me, means that we cannot be both good and evil at the same time. James explained that when a fountain is expelling sweet water, there is not salt water in it. And, vice versa, when a fountain, a.k.a. person, emits things that are brackish, or vile, how, then, can it produce good things? It's kind of like: "Do you kiss your mother with that mouth?"

I tentatively concede that **"all's fair in love and war"** is not intended to be taken literally, rather it is a rhetorical joke. Hopefully, that is so. But do we really know if teachings such as this confirm unconscious beliefs in the minds of little children? Think about it, really. Children often take to heart what adults say. Although some kids are naturally quite good at it, critical thinking skills are often under development throughout the early years. Unexamined instruction goes in and is sometimes simply believed. We hope they figure it out, but what happens if they don't? Do we end up with a bunch of Annie Wilkes running around? Food for thought.

Now I refer back to John Lyly and his marvelous satirical work, *Euphues: The Anatomy of Wit*. Is this parable, **all's fair in love and war**, still a joke? I think not. Thus, by taking this seriously, we can justify a tremendous range of misdeeds. In fact, all activity can be cleverly placed upon the spectrum which stretches between the polarized forces of love and war. In other words, it's "game on" for everything from atrocities of war crimes and torture, to uxoricide as in the story of Bluebeard (mentioned in the section entitled *Curiosity Killed the Cat*). In other words, it's "game on" for pretty much everything, wouldn't you say? Humanity is constantly living in this tremendous polarized state--the belief that one must choose either pacifism along with death, or calamity along with life Ah, there is the lie exposed. Are there no other options? Is that all there is? At the risk of public ridicule, I say that pacifism, love, and compassion equal Life. And, therefore hate, fear, and violence equal Death. I choose life.

Finally, another musical reference--I love these. Songwriters craft their ideals into beautiful coded sound, and their messages are expressed with passionate depth. The extreme duality of love and war are clearly presented in the 1983 hit by Pat Benatar, "Love is a Battlefield". Her song says it all. Interesting, this track first appeared on Benatar's album entitled *Live From Earth*. I'll just leave that there.

Chapter 2

Fight Fire With Fire

"Be great in act, as you have been in thought;
Let not the world see fear and sad distrust
Govern the motion of a kingly eye:
Be stirring as the time; be fire with fire;
Threaten the threatener and outface the brow"... The Bastard.

Ah, here's the culprit. An enigmatic character: Philip Faulconbridge. This Englishman, in yet another of Shakespeare's masterpieces, is meant to, sort of, represent Philip of Cognac (born circa 1180). Since history has somewhat ignored the real Philip, Shakespeare took great license, and nicknamed the character Philip the Bastard. More on war, fire, and Shakespeare a little later.

"Fight fire with fire" doesn't even make any sense. Too literal, Robin, you're being too literal! In my defense, why can't we say what we mean? Or, do we?

This analysis is placed within my war section for a reason. And it flows straight into some of my philosophical questions about love and revenge. First of all, let us examine a belief system about fighting.

Fight

Fight the good fight supports all of the statements, and the genesis of my meager survey (see the chapter entitled The Battlefield), about a time for war. And maybe we aren't exactly talking about atrocities here, especially since we read this instruction from Saint Paul in 1 Timothy 6:12. But how far does this command go? How do we, mere humans, decide what would classify as a good fight? We see such wide viewpoints on this. Are we fighting for the furthering of our own agenda, and our own judgements about justice or revenge?

Fight for what is right is another philosophy which is embedded into our minds from the time we are little tikes. As I have grown and entered into various forms of activism, I have realized that fighting may not be the best way. The full expression of these philosophies of mine cannot be detailed here but will require a longer document. For now, I will state that over the last decade I have changed my perspective and my approach to saving the world. I no longer consider it a battle, and I choose my vocabulary according. Turning away from the concept of "fighting" is a paradigm shift that has worked for me.

You can't fight city hall. Ha! Yet another paradox of common expressions. The first two phrases in this small section tell us one thing, and this final one presents as opposition. And here's my point. We are also told that we can catch more flies with honey than with vinegar. The modus operandi then should be cooperation, collaboration, and service. Isn't that a more effective process than fighting? Perhaps. I know many of my reading friends will disagree. We have dreams, goals, and we live out our lives while pursuing peace. But with all of these conflicting idioms and approaches bombarding our sensibilities every day, how do we know what the next step, or the preferred strategy should be? How do we quiet those outer voices and listen to our inner voice--our intuition? With all this noise, do we even have a fighting chance?

Fire

Now, what do we mean by fire? If we are talking about a real, live, blazing fire, then obviously fight fire with fire is kind of a weird thing to say. What would our heroic firefighters say? I will concede, though, that occasionally forest fires can be addressed by actually identifying specific areas, which are set ablaze as a control barrier. So, the directive is actually true, but not in the way we all use it.

So then, by fire we mean something quite different. We mean conflict, threat, and possibly even just tenacity and personality differences within our work, social, and familial groups. And remember the many, many other uses for the word fire, including the action of taking away someone's job! One time, in a television series beginning in 2004, the "actor" playing the lead role made a stylized version of this announcement quite famous: "Yoooooou're FIRED!"

So, we can indeed feel the need to fight back when we are under fire, fired up, or walking through fire. Yet I recall another reference to Holy Scripture: "I indeed baptize you with water unto repentance: but he that cometh after me is mightier than I, whose shoes I am not worthy to bear: he shall baptize you with the Holy Ghost, and with fire" (Matthew 3:11 KJVA). Now we see fire and fighting both mentioned in the Christian Bible, but in two very different contexts than we see in the title phrase of this small chapter.

William Shakespeare, in his brilliance, coined the now slightly manipulated phrase **"fight fire with fire"** within his 1595 work entitled *The Life and Death of King John*. What the playwright meant by the passage remains the same as what we mean today when we repeat the phrase: engage the enemy in the same manner which he has engaged you. And yes, Shakespeare was referring to war. The war was between England and France, and English King John was having his butt kicked by the King of France. The name of the monarch of France? Ironically, King Philip II. Another coincidence of names? Perhaps not.

Thus, the phrase of which I write, **fight fire with fire**, as so many enduring and misunderstood idioms, is coined in literature, and uttered by a fictitious character. Today it presents as a proverb. Interesting!

And here's a cool side note. At least this discovery evoked a smile and a nod from me, because of where I live. The Worcester News (UK) reported in 2016 that a special performance of the play, King John, was occurring in commemoration of 800 years since the death of King John of England, whose reign was from the end of the 12th century and into the 13th. The play is being held on the exact anniversary of his death, in the place which holds his remains: Worcester Cathedral. The announcement can be found here: https://www.worcesternews.co.uk/news/14783205.King_John_will_be_present_for_Shakespeare_in_the_cathedral/ .

Before we leave here, let us define the intent behind today's adoption of the phrase "**fight fire with fire**". Its continued use is meant to incite. It is, indeed, a call to action and, perhaps, a call to arms. We are instructed to up our game, when the opposition so demands. But, nowadays, I consider the value of that which I seek: is it truly worth fighting for? Effort is not a bad thing, but when do we analyze why a long-term battle for something that is not materializing makes sense? Where does once well-directed tenacity become an ego-based exercise, and when are we continuing to be engaged in something that truly has become inflated in its merit? How do we identify the difference between a good fight, or one on principle, or a fight which is engaged solely for the sake of winning? I ask again, how far will we go, and to what level of fire will we escalate our intent? When are we progressing, and when are we just burning down the house?

Chapter 3

The Truth Hurts

These three words demonstrate the motherload of all intent behind this book--to escape from the virtual prison. All lies, deceptions, and manipulations come from a place of fear, which binds us. I write this from experience.

The genesis of this book was an angry response to the understanding that we each play the role of the Mayan Blue Monkey. He teases, he interferes, he tricks, and he disrupts. That's what monkeys do. But this creature reveals how we trick ourselves. We lie to ourselves when we would otherwise need to admit an error and face the music. And we lie to ourselves in order to rationalize fear of stepping into our power. We hurt ourselves with agonizing judgements and arduous limitations, oftentimes created or perpetuated within our own minds. These reasons are why so many say **the truth hurts**.

But is this real? Or is "**the truth hurts**" a sneaky type of warning? Does it reinforce the error that **ignorance is bliss,** and therefore a state of naivete is a nice place to hang out? Come on--are we really telling each other that the truth is bad for us?

It's not the truth that hurts. Oh, believe me, there will be pain! But the discomfort comes along with the discovery that the truth was not visible, or worse, it was intentionally hidden from us by someone we trust. Learning that we have been deceived is excruciating.

You now may be recalling moments of clarity which occurred when another tried to deceive you. Perhaps you are smiling, and it is a humorous memory of a child who was making the attempt. I love how oblivious kids can be to the fact that we can see right through them. Some little ones are indeed quite crafty, but it can be adorable. At least it always starts out that way! Grown up lies are a different thing altogether. Suddenly it's not so funny anymore. It's never the truth causing the pain, it's the untruth! See where I'm going with this?

Relationships and careers developed out of dishonesty or corruption are like the house that was built upon shaky ground, as opposed to solid rock. I refer to Luke 6 here, in the New Testament. Everyone knows that one. Lies are the sand. Truth is the rock. It is grievous indeed to suffer the results of building upon instability. Betrayal causes invisible wounds that can be difficult to heal. That, my dear, is the painful truth.

Let's look at the bright side of this, and think of a related phrase that, once again, has ambiguous implications. A friend of mine loves to use this one: **no pain, no gain**. Another favorite of this guy is: **"Everything bad that happens is a gift"**. I'm sure you can already imagine the lively arguments that ensue--all in good humor, though! My position is this: suffering is not good. I must concede, however, that, according to legend, the Ascended Master Quan Yin intentionally endured persecution and great suffering in order to learn how to heal the suffering of others. I can understand how that should be regarded as a gift--from Quan Yin to us, and for that I am grateful. But in general, we use the phrase **"no pain, no gain"** to indicate that nothing should come easy. This is also not a belief I ascribe to. I just wanted to mention those other idioms for you to think about. I also won't contribute any more of my friend's viewpoints here--he'll have to write his own book.

Let us go back to the original statement: **the truth hurts**. As I mentioned earlier, I contend that it is not the truth that hurts, rather it is the lie that hurts. At first, when we discover that someone has deceived us, it hurts. When we discover we have deceived ourselves, it hurts. Perhaps ego comes into play here as well, just to further complicate the situation. But think chakras for a moment here.

A sudden realization of deception evokes a negative emotion, or response. Our mind, emotions, and body all react. One could even say one's heart is hurt. The lower chakras are impacted, as we may experience real or perceived threats to our security, and our power. The heart chakra is where we find healing through compassion for self, and for others--even the liars. The throat chakra, within which is our very truth center, now must process that lie into truth, in a very personal way. See the blueprint of the rising of the circumstance, through the healing energy of the chakras. The third eye will clarify, as we see with new eyes, or perhaps we see for the first time, the lie become truth. Finally, the crown is where we experience divine understanding--gnosis. This is our final destination. Thus, learning the truth is a sacred experience. Now we have released the betrayal--we are enlightened. We are free.

Part Two

Time and Money

"Who owns your time owns your mind". Jose Arguelles.

Death and taxes? No! Instead let's talk about Time and Money! But, in this section you will look at death in a new light, and you will see the role taxation has played in the development of our modern measure of time.

Unfortunately for so many of us, these two important elements of society, money and time, represent lack and shortage. We never have enough time. And the time we do have is often frantically used to create more money, which we also never seem to have enough of. Thus, we resemble, or feel like, the gerbil running in the wheel! But must it be this way? Are we doomed to continue in this manner forever, for all time? Why do we complain so much, and yet have not developed solutions? Do solutions even exist? Or is this **just the way the cookie crumbles**?

The two concepts, money and time, necessitated some pondering. Weird questions and ideas developed as I took a deep dive into these topics. There is no end to where the study of time can take us. And in the process of connecting money to this exercise, some interesting half-truths and deceptions surfaced. I can't exactly say that I found all of my answers, but perhaps you will find yours.

Time

The Harmonic Convergence of 1987 marked the beginning of an era, and a new Law of Time. Next, the December 21, 2012 prophecy brought a new measure of time. Some called 2013 a "calibration year". These theories, and several others, have certainly brought attention to an end to time as we know it, and a beginning of a new understanding: time as an instrument of peace.

Jose and Lloydine Arguelles were a visionary couple, and they authored a brilliant series of books that explained what it meant to see time from a new perspective, and a new dimension. *260 Postulates on the Dynamics of Time*, by Jose Arguelles, is a fascinating read, intended to activate a galactic mindset and multidimensional intellect. Explore these teachings online at Tortuga 13:20 (https://tortuga1320. com) and Foundation for the Law of Time (https://lawoftime.org). I guarantee it will be time well spent!

Time flies when you're having fun! But wait--is that a good thing or a bad thing? This statement indicates that our time is fleeting, elusive, and difficult to control. And within the statement is a second meaning: one disassociates with time when one is in a "happy place". What a great feeling it would be to always experience that. You see, time isn't really going any faster--it's just that we are enjoying our time. If we could achieve a heightened state of joy in our lives, and a break from the mechanics of time, we would not experience time in the same way. Yet, we are committed to limiting our joy times, and, instead, adhering to society's norm--on Monday mornings the collective workforce returns with a groan, to the drudgery of cubicle dwelling. And then, we ache in the desire that the hands on the clock whirl towards whatever time is quittin' time.

Stories to Awaken the World was written by Feng Menglong (1574-1646) and first released in 1627. Within Feng's works one may find the original version of what has become known as an ancient proverb: "May you live in interesting times". There is very little historical evidence linking this verse to Chinese prophecy, as is commonly believed. But within Feng's stories we find a hidden gem, translated (imperfectly) as: "Better to be a dog in a peaceful time, than to be a human in a chaotic period."

Chaos, within that context, referred to a historical time of instability, disaster, or war. Thus, the turning of the phrase--the *manipulation* of it--renders it a curse. "Interesting times", when matched as synonymous with "chaotic times", indicates a wish for someone to experience a less than peaceful life. Not a nice thing to wish for!

Albert Einstein (1879-1955), a German theoretical physicist had an interesting understanding of what is referred to as "block-universe" theory. This study introduces a non-linear approach to time. Combined with *260 Postulates on the Dynamics of Time*, as previously mentioned, we see synchronicity as the evidence of a new view on time.

Objective Becoming is the work of Bradford Skow, an author, philosopher, and professor. Again, we discover that humans must comprehend time in new ways. Skow indicates his agreement with block universe theory, and brilliantly defines and describes what we have been conditioned to believe as the "passing" of time. Reaching a new perspective, and realizing additional dimensions as associated with the work of Einstein, Arguelles, and Skow, we now ask why this knowledge is still largely considered theoretical. How many people know this? Why hasn't this information become more widely accepted? Are we being kept in the dark, or are we reticent in our acceptance of discoveries this conceptual? Are we lazy thinkers, linear thinkers, and stuck in our ways? Or is this truly a new time? And are we ready for a transition into nonlinear, conceptual insight? Perhaps the time is ripe.

What is the meaning behind the phrase "clean your clock"? This formidable utterance describes violence and indicates a threat of harm from one person to another. It oftentimes refers to specific violence to one's face, thus making the allegorical reference between the "face" of a clock, and that of a person. Interesting that a clock, usually identified as a time keeping device, has a dual meaning. And the word "clock", when used as a verb, means to strike, beat, or deliver a blow. Another activity we would agree is not very nice!

Here is one more provocative slogan about time: "doing time". We employ this phrase to describe the status of people who are incarcerated. These adults, and youth in many cases, have lost the freedom to make decisions about their physical body, and the location and activities that accompany such freedom. This situation is tightly bound to the concept of time--those imprisoned are no longer allowed to manage their own time. Therefore time = freedom. This statement, doing time, is also quite comparable, in its effect, to a phrase mentioned in the introduction to this book. In the Holy Bible, 1 John 1:6 (KJVA) speaks of truth as something we do--it is an activity, an action, a commitment. Is time, then, also something that we do?

Money

> Hemingway: *"I am getting to know the rich."*
> Colum: *"I think you'll find the only difference between the rich and other people is that the rich have more money."*

The full text of this teaser is found within F. Scott Fitzgerald's short story entitled "*The Rich Boy*" (1926). In paragraph 3, the author writes: "Let me tell you about the very rich. They are different from you and me. They possess and enjoy early, and it does something to them, makes them soft, where we are hard, cynical where we are trustful, in a way that, unless you were born rich, it is very difficult to understand."

So, which is it? Money is what makes us different, and what sets us apart? Remember, "what sets us apart" can also be defined as something that divides us. Perhaps Cyndi Lauper was spot on when, in 1984 she released "Money Changes Everything" --a sad and cynical message that the desire for money trumps all--even love. Could this be true? But didn't the Beatles, in 1967 remind us that "All You Need is Love"? Interesting that this latter song was featured in the Our World broadcast from England. This famous transmission was a part of the first international satellite broadcast and happened to be accompanied by some political and other controversies, including Soviet Union disapproval towards England in the aftermath the Arab-Israeli Six Day War. Although this is not meant to be a history book, the connections between these events--the conflict and the broadcast featuring the song--appear quite synchronistic. But we can move on.

Biblical references to money abound. There are hundreds, possibly thousands of interpretations of scripture regarding money. And many of us have been taught that money causes people to behave very badly. But we need money to survive in today's world. So, what, then are we to do? Perhaps we could ascribe to the beliefs in the book of Isaiah: "Ho, every one that thirsteth, come ye to the waters, and he that hath no money; come ye, buy, and eat; yea, come, buy wine and milk without money and without price. Wherefore do ye spend money for that which is not bread? and your labor for that which satisfieth not? hearken diligently unto me, and eat ye that which is good, and let your soul delight itself in fatness". (Isaiah 55:1-2 KJVA). I'll just leave that there.

Through the next few pages, the strange connections between time and money will dance before you and entice you into a puzzling realm. Ideas about selling time, wasting time, value, vice, power paradigms and other concepts are initiated. And try not to rush through this section--you have all the time in the world.

One more thing needed mention, and this is about time and ownership. The notion that "our time is not our own" flies in the face of the opening quote for this section. If Mr. Arguelles' discovery is accurate, then we now must each ask ourselves: who actually owns your time and mine?

Chapter 4

Time is of the Essence

"I'll never get those two hours back". Lots of people.

What if we knew we had all the time in the world? Would we do things differently? Would we live in a new way--and love in a new way? Removing the limitations of our hyper-scheduled 24 hours would change the game--forever.

So, what's your hurry? Our urgency is quite possibly artificially created. Combine the notion that **time is of the essence** with the belief that **we only live once**, and we become humans with an obsession to rush, to get it all done, to not waste time, and to win the race. How's that working for us? Remember Harry Chapin's wildly popular 1974 folk song entitled *Cat's in the Cradle.* In the lyrics, which were co-authored by Chapin's wife, Sandy, we hear the lamentations of a man enraptured by what turned out to be the wrong priorities, at least for him. Interesting note: this song was first produced on an album called *Verities and Balderdash.*

I have witnessed, in film, a disturbing portrayal of our unhealthy obsession with never having enough time. It was in the 2011 movie *In Time,* starring Justin Timberlake. I don't remember where I was when I first saw the movie but after about 20 minutes of watching it, I was so troubled by the premise that I stopped looking at it. The scenes in that movie have remained with me and continue to haunt me. In the film, time is literally life or death. Further, as in our real, off-screen lives, our time is not our own. Will it be as unsettling for you as it was for me? Watch the movie and decide for yourself.

When we believe that **time is of the essence**, we are set upon the Accelerated path of Achieving, Accomplishing, Advancing, Acquiring, and Amassing. Some of these elements are noble, some not so much. It depends how you look at it. Beyond the urgency of these activities, we see a common denominator--measurement. All of these milestones are understood by being monitored and measured. Can we look at these in a new way? Who sets the standards for the measurement, and who decides if we have **used our time wisely**? Humor me please, as I say let us change the rules, stop measuring, and find an undiscovered truth within the essence of time.

Think about what each of those "A" words (listed above) means to you and think about the way each of those concepts was first presented to you. Beginning in kindergarten, we are evaluated and assessed in order for our parents and teachers to determine our propensity for success. But are children, as wee little newbies, examined as divine souls? Are we looked upon as powerful energy systems, with brand new human bodies, destined to live out a sacred calling? And, more importantly, are we taught to examine ourselves--to decide for ourselves what our own personal calling is, and what the fruits of that calling will look like? The calling I speak of is, oftentimes, predetermined by an existing and powerful collective brainwashing.

How much more rapturous would life be if we each followed our own goals and dreams, from a clean slate, when each of us is ready. Instead, our life goals are programmed into us at an early age--not our personal goals, but those of our current society. Achieving, for some, might not necessarily apply to academic grades or public awards, rather it might look like a deep connection to their inner beings. Accomplishing may not represent getting a college degree (and oftentimes crippling debt that accompanies it), rather it may be an understanding of our potentials as an unlimited spirit. Advancing may mean reaching enlightenment, one joyful step at a time. You get the point.

One more note about the "A" words--how often have we sought the Accelerated route to an Achievement. We want "it" as quickly as possible. We look for shortcuts, we drive ourselves, and we gather momentum. Is this like a "drive by" lifetime? What are we missing as we zoom through the very life we hold so precious? This feels like a paradox to me. Clichés abound in this book, so I must ask why we do not follow our own advice and **take time to smell the roses**. Those who study botany, herbology, and ascribe to aromatherapy will tell us that the scent of roses is a wonderful experience to our olfactory system and shifts us closer to a state of peace. This literal science should, perhaps, be viewed as analogous to our life journeys. Give it a try and stop rushing for a moment. Look around you with fresh eyes and feel what you could be missing. Give yourself the gift of time and, just for a day, or even an hour, don't ask: "Are we there yet?"

Many have told me that my ideas are "out there", fanciful, and just plain nuts. I've been told: **"But that's just not the way things are"**. How sad.

In the study of galactic consciousness, Jose and Lloydine Arguelles present a concept of time that is at once new and ageless. In fact, according to this visionary couple, time is art. Jose Arguelles presents his theory as the formula $T(E)=Art$, Time multiplied by Energy equals Art. The work of the Arguelles' is quite complex and requires intense study, along with an open mind. Their profound teaching is one of a new and infinite experience of time. In their dream, humanity, in this material world, would unburden itself from the slavery of the Gregorian calendar and an artificial, mechanized time system. It would be a return to peace, beginning with a shift of each individual mindset.

In the section within this collection entitled You Only Live Once, you will find a companion ethos to the one espoused here. These two chapters are highly connected. If, indeed, our journeys are endless and timeless, as communicated in many ancient cosmologies, then we truly do have **all the time in the world.** Now what will you do differently?

Chapter 5

You Only Live Once

"For certain is death for the born, and certain is birth for the dead; therefore over the inevitable thou shouldst not grieve". The Bhagavad Gita, second discourse (27).

As embodied humans living a physical existence, how can we be so sure that we only live once? Some religious doctrine would tell us that this is so: there is one life on the physical plane--one span of a typical human experience on Earth. But is this really so?

What is this eternal afterlife we have heard so much about? Who has been there and back? Where are the reports from the scouts? I'll get to that.

For Christians, how can we be sure the words of Jesus verily are correctly interpreted? In fact, there is much speculation that Jesus, Himself, is the reincarnated Melchizedek. Considering that we incarnate into brand new little human bodies, live a very human, earthbound existence, experience the deterioration of our bodies, die, and then come back to do it all again requires a massive stretch of the imagination for many, many people. Others look upon that process as a no brainer. How do we bridge the expanse between the belief structure around this, and where can we find common ground?

Within the belief that **we only live once**, I have experienced

26

what I call The Five Frights. These are scary and depressing notions. Some of them are based upon cultural conditioning, and others are religious tenets.

Here is what we are taught:

1. **Life sucks and then you die**. A great many of us recognize this expression was from a comedic song, released in 1988 by a British band called Cerebral Fix. But it verbalizes an underlying, pervasive belief that we hear quite often--and we've been hearing it in one form or another and passing it down from generation to generation. This phrase is a real downer, and it takes all the fun out of being a human!

2. **Life isn't fair.** This one gets me into trouble all the time. See the expanded version of my thoughts on this one in a separate chapter.

3. **We're only human,** so that means life will be fraught with pain and suffering. This story indicates that being human is an undesirable condition. Then why are we? If we are here to suffer, then that means God made us just so He could watch us squirm? Some people even go so far as to say things like **no pain, no gain.** Well, then, what is the point of striving for something that actually causes us even more pain? And why would any of our accomplishments even matter? Are we supposed to compare who suffers the most before kicking the bucket? Must our victories be measured by how much they hurt? This is especially unpleasant for women--after all, we even **must suffer to be beautiful**!

4. **Damned if you do, and damned if you don't**. I guess we're screwed. We must be good and do the right thing in the hopes that we please God. Perhaps this mission actually makes a lot of sense, and perhaps it is a noble purpose. But how do we really know what God considers as a model of "good" behavior? We could take our cues from the holy scriptures of the world's leading religions, but for some reason that's a little

too tough--especially when we don't really agree on what the books are teaching. To tattoo, or not to tattoo. **Money is the root of all evil.** Bad girls become salt. Submission. No funny business with goats. The list is endless. I'm not trying to be sarcastic or disrespectful, but I am sure that I am not alone in feeling absolutely overwhelmed by the myriad of rules and dogma that are beyond comprehension. Yet those involved in leading organized religion, especially some pretty mainstream denominations, insist that we come into this world already in a sinful and fallen state. That sounds hopeless. But those same ministers teach that we have Jesus, the Great Counselor, who instructs us to watch and learn. And at the bottom of it all, His philosophy is pretty simple--love. All distractions aside, all we need do is love and we are all set. Yet when I turn on the news or scroll through social media rolls, I see that "Love" appears to be the most daunting directive of all. And supposedly we only get one shot. It's do or die. Sink or swim. And to quote another great leader of our time: *"There is only do, there is no try"*...Yoda.

5. **Judgement Day.** When we reach the pearly gates, we will be judged by God, our very Creator. He will then decide if we are to go to heaven or to hell--forever. Really? Forever? What does that even mean? Eternity. Does this seem reasonable? If nothing else, the Supreme Intelligence is reasonable, no? Is that the God you know? It is not my belief that some humans enjoy bliss and paradise, while others are condemned to pain and devastation....forever.

I do not intend that my personal viewpoints should insult those who believe my Five Frights. I would much rather be the subject of ridicule than one who offends. My perspective is my own, and a topic such as this necessitates acceptance of many different opinions and possibilities. I am open to all, and I hope you are too!

But please take a second look at the five points above and notice what, if any, emotions arise. Strong feelings can often be interpreted as the first signal. What these emotions may tell us is that we may need to sort something out. To me, an intense emotion associated with a theory, especially one that is religious in nature, indicates that a belief system is in place. In other words, beliefs are embedded into our value system, and become who we are. If that appears to be the case with any of the Five Frights, or any other manipulations within this book, then you have learned my lesson well. But where did this conditioning come from, and why do we feel this way when it is challenged? Finding the answers to that question could take a lifetime, or two.

A practice of considering theories while holding a sense of detachment may better enable one to decide if the theory fits their perspective. The next logical step is to determine why it's a match with your values, or why not. If detachment is not present, and anger, fear, or hate are instead present, then how does one enter into an enlightened argument? I tread lightly as I explain.

If the Christian Bible is your holy book, then look within those pages for some ambiguous teachings. What I have discovered is similar to the opening quote of this essay, from the Bhagavad Gita. Is there one life on Earth, and then another one in the afterlife? Or do we, indeed, reincarnate? Here goes:

> "That whosoever believeth in him should not perish, but have eternal life." (John 3:15 KJVA).

> "In hope of eternal life, which God, that cannot lie, promised before the world began;" (Titus 1:2 KJVA).

> "And this is the promise that he hath promised us, even eternal life." (1 John 2:25 KJVA).

The determination must now be made between earthly life, and eternal life. Unless we decide they are one and the same. Eternal life is not necessarily afterlife. Eternal means unending, forever, perpetual. Afterlife means after life. This is the ambiguity that must be reconciled.

Michael Newton makes a fascinating case for the notion of souls intentionally choosing physical embodiment. Therein is evidence of purpose. Purpose of the soul, or the reason our soul was created, presents as somewhat in opposition to religious doctrine. Religion does indeed acknowledge a soul, but it describes the human as a single created form, gifted with a unique and single soul. Dr. Newton has transcribed the reports of subjects who, while in a state of deep hypnosis, were able to describe what they experienced while between incarnations. This book is definitely worth the read. I understand that each is free to decide for themselves what it is that they believe, but the questions for me are these: do we decide to believe as part of our free will? Or do we believe because we have learned it? One thing I ask here, and throughout this entire book, is that when discerning truth from untruth, you **consider the source**.

This evasion, **you only live once,** is a dare--a double dog dare! I can get behind people saying: "**You only live once**" to entice each other to live big, meaning make life great. But perhaps our motivation for living large could come from another place: purpose. Think bigger now. Think outside the box. Think purpose of eternal soul, as opposed to purpose of a single lifetime on Earth. Instead of living frantically, trying to do good and get to heaven, what if we, again, took the view from the top. Time and lifetime are two intense and infinite concepts. We may never fully understand them, but we'll have fun trying!

Chapter 6

Time Heals All Wounds

Time heals some wounds, for sure. But there are many types of trauma that do not heal all by themselves, simply because of the passing of time. Some of these injuries are invisible, but so very real and painful.

When we have an outer injury, we address it vigorously, aggressively, and with great care. Do we do the same for emotional, or mental pain? I think not. Instead, invisible injuries are largely ignored and left to fester and infect other parts of us. Hence the phrase **time heals all wounds** is meant to justify how much we ignore the inner pain within ourselves and within each other. Some may say this is a passive approach to healing, I say it is not an approach at all.

I will go so far as to say that the very misrepresentation, **time heals all wounds**, is meant to teach us to ignore our spiritual wounds as well. Time and again, we do not seek to recognize and cure inner pain caused by some religious teachings, or misunderstandings about our spirituality. Some folks even suffer from a sense of disconnection to God. So, let us address the wounds that we generally do not see time healing. Seems absurd to me to rely on time to fix psychological, emotional, and spiritual wounds, when we treat physical wounds so diligently. Is this a blindness to the severity of these wounds? Should we not be caring for all four of our bodies: physical, mental, emotional, and spiritual? Let us look at these very human aspects and think about ways we can actively heal ourselves and each other, without waiting for the external, and abstract, concept of time to do it for us.

1. *Spiritual wounds.* As a child growing up Catholic, I was not alone in learning some pretty disturbing things about humanity. Here are a few of the highlights:

   • Eve caused the hellish existence we all must experience
   • Women must submit to and obey their husbands
   • All are born as sinners who must be washed clean
   • God commanded righteous people to murder an entire society and occupy their land
   • We each will face judgement and a possible eternity in hell

   You may have observed an overlap here, as some of these ideas are mentioned in other chapters within this book. That is because, to me, they are important concepts, and apply to multiple areas of our lives. The teachings within the previous bullet points do not feel right to me. This is not the God I know. I cannot get my head around these interpretations--they are actually quite traumatic, and I have learned that they are traumatic to many people. Who can help heal those wounds? How much time must go by before those traumas are transmuted?

   My intention is not to bash on the Holy Bible, for it remains, for me, a holy source to God, Jesus, and the true meaning of life. But the points mentioned above are devastating events and teachings for which there appears to be no cure, and no relief. Time does not heal spiritual wounds.

2. *Psychological wounds.* It is no secret that the state of mental health care in the United States is in a bad way. As people languish in emergency rooms or on waiting lists, they don't get better. When people wait on a psychiatric appointment

for months, they do not become healed while they wait. And, at the risk of sounding like a conspiracy theorist, I observe that more and more people are unable to receive treatments they deserve because of power structures that are in place. Soldiers return from battle, often wounded in many ways, and seek relief. Post-traumatic stress disorder is one issue they suffer from. This is a devastating condition for which the help available appears to be inadequate. Time does not heal psychological wounds.

3. *Emotional wounds.* Grief, rage, and fear are just a few examples of some devastating emotions. These feelings create stressors and lead to actual physical pain. Further, long-term distressing emotional states have been linked to hypertension, poor sleep habits, weight problems, self-harm, suicide, and more. These things certainly don't just clear up on their own. Time does not heal emotional wounds.

When somebody tells you that **time heals all wounds,** ask them how. How does that work? In a linear concept of time, which is a 3rd Dimensional illusion, the belief is that as the event causing the wound becomes more and more distant, the wound becomes forgotten, thus healed. I call mendacity on that one. In the words of Russian author Leo Tolstoy (1828-1910): "*What then can we do*"? So often we tell each other to get over it or move on. This can be very sound advice but where is the practical side of this advice--the how?

Going out on a limb here I would say there are hundreds of healing modalities which cover all four of our bodies: physical, mental, emotional, and spiritual. When I say hundreds, I really mean hundreds. But why are we still facing a health crisis? A little bit of quick research on our own government's website about the Center for Disease Control and Prevention, and we discover 136.9 million people presented at hospital emergency rooms, 39 million of them for injuries. Interesting that less 2.2% of these visits resulted in transfers to psychiatric hospitals. What are these numbers telling us? Admittedly, the information is vague. The website gives us some "Fast Facts" but fails to indicate a time frame. I assume the data is for one year, but I have no way of knowing that at first look. Also, I noticed some glaring ambiguities within the information provided. I won't go into the details, as this is not the intention here. But I do see where some get the feeling that we live within some conspiracies.

Is there a benefit to convincing people that wounds are healed by the passing of time? Could it be that there is such a massive revenue stream for the emergency treatment of injuries and illnesses, that's where the industry leaders are focused? And with domestic revenue around half a trillion dollars, are the pharmaceutical companies making more money by keeping people sick than by making them well? I digress here, but my point is this: is the health and wellness industry addressing only issues where treatment is profitable? And the rest are told to wait it out? Come on—I can't possibly be the only one who has come up with this.

This chapter started out because I get pissed off when someone says **time heals all wounds**. Yes, time heals some wounds, but certainly the overwhelming majority of wounds are not healed by time alone. They are healed by first acknowledging the various mental, emotional, and spiritual wounds that cause or exacerbate many physical health issues. Then we get to the healing work. We love, we listen, we learn, and we apply the hundreds of modalities that are available to us. However, alternative therapies and holistic healing practices may not be the low-hanging fruit that corporations profit from. Hence the conditioning that these ideas won't work. As paranoid as this may sound, are we taught to ignore deep trauma so it *will* manifest into measurable physical disease, which can then be treated by the medical community? Or is it simply that the unseen wounds are still mysterious, and cures are of yet undiscovered and undeveloped? Come on, you don't really believe that, do you?

Call me crazy, but please don't ever tell someone who is grieving, or who suffers from PTSD that time heals all wounds. Depending on who you say it to, you may end up with an E.R. visit yourself!

Chapter 7

Time is Money

When we meet somebody for the first time, we often ask them: "What do you do?" Translation: "How do you make money?"

Why? Why is that information so important to us, and why is it consistently the first thing we seek to discover about newbies? It would be fantastic if, when asked what one does, one would respond with excitement and reveal: "I hike mountain trails", or "I make pottery", or "I watch cartoons". What if the response could be "I volunteer at the homeless shelter every other weekend", or "I sponsor a child in a developing country", or even "I love"? Are those types of answers simply not interesting enough? Why not? Are we so programmed that we classify each other based solely upon how we each sell our time?

"**Time is money**" does indeed sometimes apply, yet only during the process through which one sells (or purchases) time. This may sound odd, but the concept of slavery is lurking somewhere within this phrase. Also, look for an element of misguided "want" versus "need" attitudes. Jump into my paradigm for a few moments and see what I see. Envision modern American society as a nation of people enslaved to a particular viewpoint on money, especially as it relates to commerce. In the powerful belief system that **time is money,** we fuse together two elements that could be, and should be, independent of each other. Thus, the dependency between time and money sets the tone for a culture with a singular mindset.

Let us expand for a moment and understand the difference between want and need. In 1973, an inventor at Motorola, Inc. executed the first mobile telephone call. The rest, as they say, is history. Today, people are quite dependent upon mobile phones. Now, the ability to access or own a mobile phone has migrated from a desire into a necessity. Some experts even go so far as to say that people, including children, are now displaying signs of technology addiction, and are experiencing some negative behavior patterns and symptoms attributed to an overindulgence of screen time. Where is this world going?

I know that last segment was kind of a "jumping on the bandwagon" kind of rant, so I should find more examples of the blurring of "wants" and "needs". Let's see--there's men and sex. No, no--too hostile. What about a much more important topic: the Wal-Mart mentality? This term is still under definition, but, in my humble opinion, Americans desire so many material items, they are willing to perpetuate global slavery and labor trafficking in order to procure those items as inexpensively as possible. The argument--products available through fair-trade supply chains are just way too expensive. Really. Can I just stop here?

Another reason to liken the **time is money** theory to slavery is because, in the antithesis of it, time is freedom. And, money is freedom. When we control our own time, we are free. When we control our own money, we are free. When someone else controls one, or both of those precious gifts, we are no longer free. Thus, enter the third force--power. When, and why, did time become synonymous with money, and how does the quest for power come into play? As we continue to evolve deeper into a culture of capitalism and corporate mentality, we learn that those who control the time, and control the money, also have control of the power. But is this truth, or is it illusion? I envision the three elements of power, money, and time as such: think of a tripod, having three ingots, or "stakes".

Time.

2080 hours. As cognitive understanding develops, children see their parents selling time. We are driven to constantly convert our time into money. Our time is a commodity, it is for sale, and we are obsessed with its value. We teach our young students that they must determine how, when adulthood arrives, they will sell their time, every day, for a lifetime, to someone else. Those who do not exchange their time for money are shunned by society and are oftentimes unable to function "normally" in such a world where money equals our very survival. But ponder this concept now--people spend human lifetimes selling time. And the fact that some are purchasers of time indicates that it has value, however subjective that value may be. Further, we have been disillusioned to believe that the time of some humans is more valuable than the time of other humans. The question arises: does this feel natural to you?

Mastering the concept of time management is considered a critical essential skill for all. Thousands of courses are available, and books, all created by experts in time management. The driving force continues to be the understanding that becoming a more productive human makes your time more valuable. This is true under the contemporary circumstances. But what are we missing? Once again, we work to increase the monetary value of our service to another, which value remains, quite often, still subjective and largely (or completely) influenced by the employer. Where's the joy in that?

12 months. The Gregorian calendar was implemented into global society by the Vatican and is originally based upon government taxation schedules. Remember, Catholics, at that time, were the ruling political force as well as the only authorized religious system. What the Gregorian calendar also served to do (under the guise of a unifying time system), was to mask its disruptive intentions towards all things feminine. The intended result of this: a rejection of the 27-29-day moon cycle, which, through God's creation, corresponded to the natural menstrual cycle of all women. Women access enormous power

during a full moon, and this presented as a threat to the patriarchal society. A new moon energy offers innate potentials that women employ. As the cycle progresses, intuitive women create and manifest wonderful things for their families and communities. Hence the term "lunatic" (which now means "crazy person", a.k.a "woman").

Yet hope remains! There is a fascinating movement around the world, championed by people who believe that the original 13 Moon Mayan Calendar should replace our current 12-month system. This movement is called Calendar Referendum Initiative and information can be found here: https://13months28days.info/ This organization has quite an interesting mission. Those who believe in calendar reform seek a new way of thinking. Further, this movement is accompanied by conceptual learning--a higher dimensional mindset as a means to achieve world peace.

Money

Money itself is a power structure created by mankind. The idea that time is money is also a human construct. We see the most dire poverty in countries where political strife, government corruption, and war have been the norm. And we see poverty in "developed" countries such as the United States, but in an entirely different context. As mentioned, direct ownership of a patch of Gaia, Mother Earth, holds tremendous value. Landowners have historically held all of the power, as they are in control of our very planet. Truth? Truth in the worldly sense, considering that humans are anchored to earth through gravity. But what of a higher truth? Where did the permission to own pieces of our planet come from? Who created the planet? Isn't that the rightful landowner?

Power

Do you now see what I see? Power becomes the third leg of the stool. Without one of the elements which we have established as interdependent--time, money, and power, then what a different world we would see. As it stands now, stakeholders, or power brokers to some, must desperately fight to maintain their position. Otherwise, the whole structure comes crashing down. This system truly is a house of cards, and we painstakingly maintain it each and every day.

But, for me, the lifestyle of servant leadership comes to mind here. Additionally, I ponder concepts that equate power with benevolence, self-mastery, inner peace, and a transcendence of material lusts. Measuring, competing, and comparing are unimportant. I dream of the Bodhisattva Vows, of enlightenment, of heaven on Earth, and of love. Time, money, and power are no longer considered as difficult necessities, which result in a slavery to systems. Instead, as we enter the Psychozoic Era, money, power, and time are the tools to create art, peace, understanding, deeper human connection, and access to divine power--love.

Chapter 8

It Takes Money to Make Money

What a dreadful thing to tell somebody! I imagine it is an especially harmful teaching for those born and raised in poverty. As if this misstatement isn't bad enough, are we actually referring to money here? Perhaps there is a more iniquitous intention behind this. Don't worry, I'm not going to cite case studies of those who started out broke and figured out how to amass wealth. That would be boring. You and I both know those stories are out there.

Our very understanding of money, as formed from birth, is a bit confusing. We are taught that **it's all about the money**, and the race is on to be super successful and uber rich. Yes, often people will say that **money isn't everything**, but from the way we all behave, I beg to differ. So, let us talk about this and other paradoxes and why we say one thing, but we do another.

And who actually says that ridiculous phrase: **it takes money to make money**? I've heard it a bazillion times, and mostly from one type of person—one who uses it as an excuse for being broke. I guess misery likes company (that one's true). I have occasionally heard this distortion from one or two successful people, who were born into wealth. I guess they believe they are just part of the lucky sperm club.

So, yes, many people may truly believe that wealth is only ever created and/or expanded through those who already have it. This notion is obviously untrue, and by constantly telling each other this bad news, we establish a caste system type of belief. And the expectation for, or the expectation of, the poor is that they will, because they should, remain poor. Did you follow all of that? It's a little bit like saying the rich get richer and the poor get poorer. "But that really happens", you may say. And perhaps sometimes it does. But is it, at least in part, due to mental and social conditioning? That's where I'm going with this.

There is a notion called "seed money". I love plant analogies so I'm going to run with this one. Seeds propagate botanical life. Seed money, therefor, should propagate wealth--and it often does. Sometimes seeds are not viable, or lousy growing conditions result in death for the intended plant life (metaphor here). But, with the correct conditions, the organisms grow into mature, and new seed-bearing, manifestations. For example, on my kitchen windowsill is a box with about a dozen tiny, adorable lemon trees--each grown from a seed. Fruit trees eventually yield a plethora of fruit, which falls to the ground to propagate new life, and new fruit. Why is this story relevant? I'm proving the theory of seed money. However, what happens next, in our financial world, is quite unnatural and oh so human, when compared to the botanical kingdom.

You see, plants and food bearing trees produce, and also can be propagated. Seed money, which grows and bears a harvest, can also be propagated. But how often do we see that happen? I don't want to forget all of the wealthy people who do wonderful things for society--foundations, scholarships, micro-loans, etc. Thank you! But isn't there enough money in the world to end poverty? Aren't there so many bumper crops, that we could propagate enough seed money for everyone? I believe it is so. Then what happens to the harvest?

Suddenly we are told that money doesn't grow on trees! Ha ha ha. What a funny paradox! So, let us go into the recesses of our minds here, to speak of consciousness. On this planet, among us humans, I see two types of consciousness: wealth consciousness and lack consciousness. And here's where it gets weird.

Thousands of people, perhaps hundreds of thousands, ascribe to the belief that our minds control our own life outcomes. We seek to hear and speak phrases that run counter to the idea that **it takes money to make money**. "What you think about, you bring about" is a common one. And there are many very popular books and organizations that teach just that.

Think and Grow Rich, by Napoleon Hill

The Secret, by Rhonda Byrne

Ask and it is Given, by Esther and Jerry Hicks

There are hundreds of such teachings available today. I'm only scratching the surface of this theory. Experts say (and we know they're experts because they're rich) that it's all a mindset and we need only clear our emotional blocks, our wrong belie fs about our worth, and our money traumas. What is a money trauma, you ask? How about somebody telling you **it takes money to make money** for starters!

Perhaps now we can look at seed money a little differently. Maybe the understanding that each of us is powerful enough to make something (wealth) out of nothing (lack) is the true seed, And, like the mustard seed in the book of Luke, in the New Testament, perhaps our seedlings will wax into something great. Yes, yes--I know we've been told **not to count our chickens before they hatch**, but why not? Given the idea that the power to live an abundant life is all within our own thoughts and minds, isn't expectation everything?

Chapter 9

Everyone Has Their Price

How cynical we have become! How shallow! Is this true? Really?

What, exactly, are we selling? What are we willing to relinquish, if the price is right? Some say that humans are even willing to sell their souls to the devil. Please do not brush this off. "**Everyone has their price**" is an immeasurably destructive belief. Look deeper into the insinuation. This deception is all about temptation and envy. It is about greed, and hedonistic desire. Don't be fooled--this statement is a false proverb, and it serves as a very subtle reinforcement of the notion that humans are weak and will always succumb to their lusts.

Like many debilitating beliefs, "**everyone has their price**" has become yet another self-fulfilling prophecy. And when, exactly, is the prophecy fulfilled? The lie becomes truth precisely in the moment the following accompaniment is accepted: **humans are flawed**. This, now, is a defining moment--we now measure, and place a value consideration upon our very lives. Am I making too big a deal out of this one? Dearest reader, are you smiling, shaking your head, and thinking I've gone off the rails? I know you will bear with me and keep reading.

If you really want something, how far are you willing to go in order to get it? And if someone else has something you want, how low will they go? And let us assume, with hope, that this is all for a win-win outcome. But is it? This inaccuracy is quite often used during a real estate transaction, and rightly so. How motivated is the seller? The agents analyze, look for tells, and play the bidding game. This is a *material* transaction, and it is most definitely a significant one. Some things truly are **all about the money**.

But think now about transactions outside of the realm of property and flea markets. Where else are people bargaining for the most advantageous outcome? Politics? Relationships? Sports? Careers? Are we buyers or sellers? What's the value of what we have, compared to the value of what we want? What is the cost, or the price, of our lives?

The Devil's Advocate is an interesting, albeit somewhat creepy, film about a family of attorneys led by the patriarchal Satan himself. This film is all about selling out. And it's about selling one's soul to the devil in order to attain material wealth, status, lots of sex, and power. Early in the film, a trial is underway. A neophyte defense attorney represents an accused child molester. Suddenly, the freshman lawyer has a vision. The young man's insight enables him to see the path that "selling out" will lead him down. What a powerful lesson.

"Everyone has their price" teaches us that, underneath it all, lurks a lack of ethics, for all people. The implication is this: in the end material lust will prevail over morality. Thus, we learn that there are none with pure heart. None will cling to their values and walk the straight and narrow path no matter what temptations arise. Now we enter a philosophical argument--values have value, or values are valuable. According to an online definition*, value, as a noun, means the following:

> relative worth, merit, or importance:*the value of a college education; the value of a queen in chess.*

> monetary or material worth, as in commerce or trade:*This piece of land has greatly increased in value.*

---

* https://www.dictionary.com/browse/value

the worth of something in terms of the amount of other things for which it can be exchanged or in terms of some medium of exchange.

equivalent worth or return in money, material, services, etc.:*to give value for value received.*

This tells us nothing about values as a moral compass. I had to click the <u>see more </u>button and scroll down to definitions 10 and 11 in order to find value defined sociologically or ethically. Significant? Perhaps.

Dreamers like me refuse to believe that **everyone has their price**. Instead, I look to those who stood, and who continue to stand, firm in their beliefs, and refused to sell out. From Jesus to Nelson Mandela; from Pussy Riot to Anthony Borges of Parkland Florida, we find those who staunchly embody their values. Seek, and you will find examples of great leaders--but look within your own circle, too. Identify those who hold a position of trust, and who you and others can always count on for sound advice, good solutions, and selfless perspectives. Thus, in the rejection of the malicious lie, **everyone has their price**, temptation now becomes redemption.

And further, let us now consider a reversal of our perception of ourselves. A large population of humans focus on the state of humanity as the single truth of who we are. We are often taught it boils down to this: one life, a soul that is not our own, a final judgement, and then the relegation of our spirit to a good place or a bad place, forever. But another large group of people share the notion that we are divine souls, and we choose to create, and exist in, human bodies. This changes everything. We just remediated an absurd belief that souls are for sale. Liberation, or, once again, redemption, accompanies this concept. We are no longer slaves to our humanity, rather our human form becomes a symbol of our soul, and our soul's creative freedom. And these souls, yours, mine, and everyone's, are not for sale.

Chapter 10

There's No Such Thing as a Free Lunch

This one is a real whopper and is meant to discourage people from freely giving or receiving blessings. What a sad state of affairs. **There's no such thing as a free lunch** informs the population that all possess fully engaged ulterior motives when giving or receiving. "Not me", you say! I hope not. Because this fable is closely connected to gifts. And gifts are awesome things that we love to give and receive, right? Presents are meant to make others feel good, and the intent is supposed to be pure and unconditional. And, that is supposed to include gifts from God. When one believes **there's no such thing as a free lunch,** one believes some very awkward things:

1. For every gift you receive, there is an expectation (the giver's) attached. This represents the very essence of the falsehood. Haven't we been taught, from very early on, about these strings that are attached? At the very least, there is an expectation that the giver will hear the words "thank you". This habit is all about simply being polite, and we always mind our manners in civilized society. But what if the "something" that was given is problematic for the receiver? Doesn't matter.

The expectation remains. And, even beyond the act of voicing gratefulness, the recipient is even expected to *feel* a certain way. Haven't you heard that you can't buy love?

2. You have been given a gift, but a debt comes along with it. This can be thought of as next level expectation (as mentioned above in the first section). Here, the receiver is not just expected to do something in return, rather they are required. Sometimes the debt is clear, sometimes it is implied. Perhaps it is even imagined. Depending upon the circumstances, feelings often arise when we receive from others--feelings of inadequacy, joy, suspicion, relief, connection, guilt, or even validation. Which reminds me of getting a salary raise (and I know a raise is definitely not a gift). Studies show the possibility that men make more money than women because they are better at asking for it. A raise, for women, is oftentimes received along with some of the less desirable emotions just listed (suspicion, guilt). For men, a salary increase is more often accompanied by the positive ones (connection, validation).

3. You give to others, but you project your expectations upon the recipients. Around here, panhandlers on the streets are a cause for much debate. To give or not to give. "Are they scammers?" "They're just going to buy beer". And my personal favorite: "**Charity begins at home**" --this one has its own chapter within this book. But back to the street level donations. What happens here is that the person handing out a donation places restriction on what can (or should) be done with the meager cash gift. Often, since there is no confirmation that the gift will be used in exactly the way the giver expects it to be used, then, one may decide not to give.

This divisive topic has gone so far, we now watch, and admonish each other for giving, and for not giving.

4. Every act of giving or receiving is a transaction--EVERY one. Thus, this phrase, **there's no such thing as a free lunch**, is a well-intended warning. If you receive something from another, you must be wary, and suspicious of the giver's motives. Such a pervasive anxiety--to always feel compelled to question the motive drives of everyone we are connected to. Exhausting!

How far does the "**no such thing as a free lunch**" deception go? Does it reach beyond our earthly experience straight to Source? It most certainly does! Here's where we further discuss God. Are His gifts to us, those in the forms of talents, aptitudes, passions, and abundance really given with strings attached? Or are they truly unconditional, from an endless source, and infinite? Even our very gift of life is oftentimes a source of mystery and uncertainty.

Quite often children are raised with a teaching that one day, all will stand before God to receive judgement. And, Saint Peter will then be instructed as to whether or not he should open the pearly gates. Many of us carry that angst within our hearts throughout our entire lifetime. Thus, our constantly impending physical death creates an apprehension that can be quite overwhelming.

Yet, children are also taught that God is our loving Creator, our omniscient Source, and the unconditional giver of life and love. We learn, through some teachings, that we are fashioned by a pure, compassionate, and benevolent force, and that we are children of the Most High. I'm always in danger of going off on a tangent when this subject arises, so I will stop here. The point is, the two teachings (Judgement Day and unconditional love) appear, at least to me, to be misaligned and contradictory.

Moving on now, I understand that we could cite plenty of examples where a gift was *refused*, or *rejected* by the recipient because of the obvious strings attached. I've been there myself (but I won't mention any names). And I do acknowledge the pervasive practice of giving "guilt gifts", which are presented in order to extract forgiveness from another. These unpleasant exchanges demonstrate what I have referred to, twice now, as "strings". In the process of giving or receiving, we bind ourselves to each other.

But do those unbalanced experiences need be accepted as the norm? Who will imitate Atropos, and make the cut—not the thread of life, mind you, but the unintended ties that bind us in debt to each other? Even The Boss, in his 1980 release of "Ties That Bind", tries to convince another that we are all inextricably connected. His words resound as a lament--a human condition beyond our control. Is this real? Shall we, instead release this attitude and replace it by manifesting a flow of unconditional generosity, drawn from our Infinite Source? What, really, have we got to lose?

In all seriousness there is a greater, profound lesson to be learned as we ponder the truth of this calumniation, as it applies to a great portion of humanity. Examine the emotions that come along with saying and believing **there's no such thing as a free lunch**. Does this feel right to you? My hope is that we overcome this attitude and erase it from our hearts and minds. Are you with me? Here's a good place to start.

One of the most powerful tenets of Buddhism teaches detachment. Specifically, some Buddhist teachings equate attachment and pain. Thus, when we hold a reciprocal expectation during an act of giving and receiving, it hurts us. There's a word in Sanskrit that means grasping, clinging, or attaching. The word is Upādāna, which also has a literal translation of "fuel". But in the spiritual practice, the former definition goes quite deep.

Also described, within Buddhist texts, are detailed types of attachment, or clinging. These types include the habits of hanging on to rituals, physical pleasure, beliefs about oneself, and, believe it or not, erroneous viewpoints. Imagine that. If I'm getting this right--wink, wink--then the practice of believing something that is wrong can, and does, hurt us. So please don't be clingy!

I don't need to cite a bazillion examples to prove that "**there's no such thing as a free lunch**" is old saw. Look around you and see the millions of good things that millions of people do for one another, every single day. It takes only one act of unconditional giving to render this maxim fake news. Today and every day, I will take actions to debunk this erroneous viewpoint. And I'm happy to know I won't be the only one doing so.

Seek, and start to notice the free lunches everywhere. As you do so, your perspective will change. See all the loving acts of giving without condition. And see others receive gifts, without placing artificial conditions on the giver. So the next time you go out for lunch, please purchase an extra Whopper (get it), and give it to somebody for free- -with no strings attached. Prove me right!

PART 3

CHANGE

Cats, dogs, and monkeys? You may notice more than a few animal references within this book. Beginning with the leopard, animals appeared to me as spirit guides throughout the assembly of these ideas. Animals change. And they do it quite naturally. Hermit crabs move into larger shells as they grow, snakes shed their skin on a regular basis, caterpillars morph into butterflies, and so on. Do they warn each other that change will be challenging? Do the crabs dread the necessity to shop for new real estate? Are they fearful, and resist growth and development along their journeys? Do they worry what the neighbors will think? Or is that stuff just for us humans?

What can we learn from nature, and our animal guides, about change? First, we learn a multitude of untruths, and animals are used for backup. **"Curiosity killed the cat"**, **"all bark and no bite"**, and **"hear no evil, speak no evil, see no evil"** all attempt to persuade us of something. We call lawyers "snakes in the grass", and we describe ourselves as being "as happy as pigs in poop". Tall tales are "for the birds"! When you really think about it, this book is largely about parroting--the practice of repeating. Isn't that exactly what I've been complaining about? Animal analogies are everywhere, even ones that include ants, so I am running with this theme!

Did you know unicorns are in the bible? Yet we are told there's no such thing. Perhaps there was such a thing and they are now extinct. Perhaps we have simply changed the name: the modern-day Indian rhinoceros, a.k.a. rhinoceros unicornis. Really! I'm not making this up. This document is not intended to be a bestiary, but there you have it: we are expected to believe hogwash such as "**you can't teach an old dog new tricks**". And we are ridiculed for believing in unicorns, which are mentioned, more than once, in a very popular holy book.

Since nature is in the spotlight, think about the seasons, the plant cycle, and the death/rebirth of the biosphere. These are inevitable changes--effortless, unquestioned, often unnoticed. Also occurring are monumental changes: global warming, wildfires, earthquakes, and tsunamis. Earth changes, all by herself. And, yes, I said "global warming". This term has been edited to "climate change". And the terminology is different not because the circumstances are different, it's just that people couldn't get behind experts figuring out that global warming is actually happening. Because of a shortage of critical thinking, or people not taking the time to actually do some independent research, environmental scientists decided, on a global scale, to relabel it. So, global warming hasn't changed, just the name for it has changed.

In this upcoming section, you will see a whole bunch of disempowering fish stories about the nature of change. While attending a personal development seminar, I recall hearing the instructor reinforce the belief that **change is hard**. I disagree. While we may find ourselves repeating unproductive or unsatisfying behavior patterns, we can fix that. Don't get me wrong--rewiring the channels of thought in your brain may take some effort, but it should not be considered an overwhelming or near-impossible undertaking.

First one must desire, or recognize the need for, a new paradigm. Then, with focused intention one can alter the outdated and naive understandings. This practice is not something to be dreaded, rather it is a liberating process, like the blossoming of a lotus flower, bringing a new and exciting outlook. Change is fun! So, back to the development conference: a large audience, each attendee having paid lots of money to participate in this seminar, came with the intention of making powerful personal changes. By stating, early on, **that change is hard**, it seemed to me that the "expert" was *disempowering* everyone that came to him for help.

What if we now begin to welcome all of life's transformative events? What if we celebrate the notion of motion? Let us begin by remembering that each sunrise brings with it a brand new day, different from the one before. That's a natural change--today is different, and each moment is brand new. This may appear as a paradox, but we transform through presence. This book has mentioned theories of attachment or clinging. Resistance to change can be painful and self-defeating. Fear of change is just that--fear. When we remain present, as an observer, we learn. Thus, the observation, the learning, the understanding, and the new thought form is the change.

So, here's a common phrase that I actually believe: "Be the change you want to see". I love this one. It is a quote credited to the fabulous Mahatma Gandhi, and it is empowering, positive, and inspiring. How do we "be" this change? Back to focused intention.

In my first book, *Pray Without Ceasing*, I wrote a chapter about setting intention, and another chapter about focus. These two forces, when put into action, create a human powerhouse! Focus and intent are two synergistic elements that any and all humans can engage. We are born with these capabilities. We can access them at any time. Don't try to sell me on the limitations, because I'm not buying. Anyone can set an intention, and anyone can find a way to remain fixed as they manifest the intention into a new reality. And when the manifestation occurs, we have accomplished a good and successful change. This process--focused intention--creates change for the better, and it is unlimited.

Sir Anthony Weldon (1583–1648) was an Englishman and a fairly controversial political personality. He is loosely credited as being the author of *The Court and Character of King James II*. Within this text we find an interesting statement. It reminds me of something that begins as "fool me once". Sound familiar? No? Well here's another case of a piece of literature becoming manipulated into a weird proverb. I refer to a segment in the aforementioned book, on page 52: "*The Italians having a Proverb, 'He that deceives me once, its his fault; but if twice, its my fault.'*" Always the Italians!

"For once deceiv'd, was his; but twice were mine" is found in *The Iliad* (8th Century B.C.), by Homer (as translated by Alexander Pope). And if you search enough, you will also see the English, the Germans, and the Japanese even take credit for this strange figment.

Why is "**fool me once, shame on you, fool me twice, shame on me**" included here, in a section about change? Bear with me, please. This entire book is written in the spirit of uncovering distortions and misrepresentations. The genesis of this work was the desire to express the destruction that lies and misinformation can cause. I don't cite the "**fool me once**" proverb with either support of, or opposition to it. Rather I wish to remediate the moniker of "fool" as it is applied to those who have been wronged. Once again, we see the victim held accountable to change his or her outlook, and thus accommodate those who would trick. Failing to trust after being fooled once, eliminates all hope of employing the benefit of the doubt. See where I'm going here?

And who doesn't love The Who? The art of this band is laden with cynical wisdom, and the truth behind power structures and systemic oppression. Their ire is clear, as is the level of mistrust that accompanies the realizations they sing about. The lyrics of the 1971 release of "Won't Get Fooled Again" tell a gloomy tale. The cyclical nature of trust and mistrust is explicitly communicated, and **the more things change the more they stay the same** is the overarching message. Again, you may exclaim that this is true! Perhaps you're right. Let us explore this point on a different page.

For now, and from now on, don't let the naysayers get to you.

Analyze every word that is said to you. Trust your intuition. Let the cat out of the bag! Keep your eyes on the prize. Change as often as you like, or don't if you don't want to! Don't be swayed and definitely don't be fooled into thinking you can't! Go ahead and move that mountain already!

Chapter 11

A Leopard Can't Change Its Spots

"Can an Ethiopian change his skin or a leopard its spots? Neither can you do good who are accustomed to doing evil." (Jeremiah 13:23 NIV).

This analogy gives us extremely valuable information: people can't change. But can they? And don't they? Have we not heard miraculous and heartwarming stories of people who have turned their lives around? How hopeless to believe that we are incarnated into an existence which is completely beyond our control--to suffer or to flourish, according to the will and design of a powerful creative force separate from ourselves.

Saint Paul is a leopard who most intentionally changed his spots. Originally Saul of Tarsus, we learn of this man in Acts of the Apostles, when he approved and witnessed the execution of Stephen, a loving and faith-filled evangelist. Saul, a learned Pharisee, was happy to guard the coats of the men who carried out Stephen's murder. And Saul is described as a man hell-bent on destroying the fledgling church of Jesus. "As for Saul, he made havoc of the church, entering into every house, and haling men and women committed them to prison". (Acts 8:3 KJVA).

But something happened to Saul, while travelling to Damascus in search of Christians to persecute. He fell ill, became blind, and he and his companions heard voices. For days he was blinded and bedridden. But Saul's sight was restored and his spirit, was healed by Anani´as, a follower of Jesus. After this miracle, and with a changed name (as is fitting for a changed man), Paul became a dedicated leader of the new church, as established by Jesus. But this conversion required Paul to change his ways, denounce his past, and earn the trust of those he had persecuted. These undertakings required humility, hard work, sacrifice, and a new vision for himself. Against all odds, Paul had transformed. He was a radically different person.

There exist innumerable stories similar to that of Saint Paul's conversion. Hundreds, or perhaps thousands of women and men released from prison have become ministers and youth mentors. And even less dramatically, let us look within our own families and within our circles of acquaintances for examples of those who have become changed. Alcoholism and drug addiction are areas where we see radical changes in many, many people who succeed at recovery. In the time of this opioid crisis, we all can find those who rose from the ashes as the Phoenix, and became a renewed person. Think about it. And then ask--how does this happen and where do we start?

Let's talk about our junk. Junk DNA, to be specific. These non-coding sections of human genomes have no function. And there are lots of these sequences. Did you know this? I wonder if it is reasonable to accept that so much of our chemistry, within these structures, is truly there for nothing. Consider for a moment that this "junk" DNA has an undiscovered purpose. Or worse, consider that humans have been deceived into believing that parts of their bodies have no function at all. Some theories offer that these specific genome sequences are meant to perform ancient and forgotten functions. Some believe that our DNA is encoded with an infinite amount of universal information, meant to inform our bodies, our minds, and even our souls. Could it be possible that modern science refuses to acknowledge the esoteric potentials within our blueprints? What if the theory of self limitation is illustrated and applies here--**we are our own worst enemy**?

A journey into the mystery behind non-functioning DNA can also lead us to a modality called psychoneuroimmunology. This concept makes distinct and powerful connections between our emotions, our mental state, and our physical health. According to some, each of us has the ability to reprogram, adjust, and heal our very cells through the processes of faith and pure, focused intent. Thus, we can heal ourselves of disease, slow down the aging process, and even correct chronic health issues. All of this is done through direct communication with your own cells, using an innate mind process. There are many documented cases of amazing recoveries and spontaneous remission of disease which are unexplainable by the medical community. Are those the outliers? Or are they the examples of what is possible? So here is where we discern the lies from the truth--do we continue to remain closed off from our very life process itself? Do we even truly understand our own electrons, and our own cell division process? Do we trust the medical and pharmaceutical communities and therefore don't need to know the detail of our own bodies? Or do we already know, albeit largely unconsciously, and have the ability to control our own functions? Can we actually change ourselves from deep inside--at a subatomic level? If this is true, then could we not believe that, just possibly, the leopard could change as well?

I know that people can and do change. I've seen it. Those who use the deception **"a leopard can't change its spots"** really mean to say that change is impossible. Those are the same people who would have us believe that **change is hard**. What a discouraging thing to say--to yourself and others.

And since we are using animal totems in this section, don't forget the parallelism to **a leopard can't change its spots: you can't teach an old dog new tricks**. This manipulation applies in the same manner and is most definitely refuted by the examples of Saint Paul and other unnamed thousands of leopards. Whether it be a dog or a leopard, change is possible, and we see it every day--one just needs to look for it.

Since childhood and, more powerfully, since the onset of the assembling of this book my leopards have transformed. Some of them have gone from gold or white with black spots to a new shade of blue--a hue I have not seen before. My symbolic leopard morphs, he basks in his newness, and he becomes different for me each day, as the ever-changing horse of a different color in L. Frank Baum's timeless and brilliant creation, *The Wonderful Wizard of Oz*. Look at the leopards all around you. What do they look like? Are they blue, like mine? Have they changed? Are they different somehow? Look at them in a new way, and they may appear changed to you. Look again. Look tomorrow and again next week. Observe the changing spots of humans on their journeys through life. I see it. Don't you? After all, **perception is reality**, is it not?

Chapter 12

Change is Hard

I get a lot of flak for this one.

In the title chapter A Leopard Can't Change its Spots, you'll find some viewpoints on changeability, most especially the transformations of people like Saint Paul. Let us think about a similar process, and another reluctant prophet, in the book of Jonah. Like Saint Paul, God gave Jonah a directive and told him: we can do this the easy way, or we can do this the hard way. There, my friends, is the kernel of truth within the concept of change--it is only hard if we make it so!

In the Christian faith, there is a practice called Baptism. Parents present their child at their place of worship, announce their vows before God and the congregation, and then they watch while the child's sin is washed clean away. According to Saint Paul himself, this little person is actually "a new creature". This practice is also extended to adults, who, upon emerging from the baptismal pool, are considered born again. This practice, and the explanation of it, are quite clear throughout the New Testament, beginning with our introduction to John the Baptist. When one comes to Christ, one has passed through a miraculous and profound change. "Therefore if any man be in Christ, he is a new creature: old things are passed away; behold, all things are become new." (2 Corinthians 5:17 KJVA). How easy is that?

Let us examine the paradoxes of change. In examining the phrase

change is hard, I began to see *some* changes as hard. Yet other changes appeared as easy, and, oftentimes quite welcomed. So, to blithely espouse that **change is hard** demonstrates that we have missed the mark and are hereby rendering *all* change as something to be avoided. I call this idea The Opposing Nature of Change--Natural Change and Unnatural Change. By convincing ourselves that all **change is hard**, we install a force of resistance against the whole lot, most of which is natural and quite beneficial. What a ridiculous thing to do!

The phenomena of Natural Change consist of things that change in a way that is easy to accept--events that bring us joy such as a salary raise, a new relationship, a child, growth from childhood to young adulthood, etc. These are the inevitable transformations, or the betterments which occur along the journey through a life that is constantly transforming, quite naturally. Natural changes can bring possibilities, synchronicities, and opportunity.

But as humans age, their bodies begin to lose vitality. This is considered to be an undesirable, or hard change, albeit a natural one. The change itself, instead of being labelled as "hard", is instead considered unwelcome. Aging is not a difficult change, per se, to *make*, as we don't actually *do* anything. Rather, it is a difficult change to *accept*.

Recently, I learned something interesting. Another natural change, although quite rare, is the potential that an individual's blood type can change. This is something that is not well known outside of the scientific/medical community, but it's there. This change happens because of an occurrence within the body: malignancies, bone marrow transplants, autoimmune disease, and even infections can cause a person's blood type to change. Again, I mention this because this change, like other natural changes mentioned, does not require action--it just happens.

Unnatural changes, or changes that *appear* to be unnatural, are more difficult to accept. Here is where we enter the realm of intention, effort, and disruption. Changes within this category may include breaking bad habits; transforming learned, limiting beliefs; losing weight; improving one's countenance; considering new perspectives;

and the like. Are these naturally occurring changes? --no. Good changes? --absolutely. Hard? --that's up to you. Here is where we stop saying **change is hard**, breathe a sigh of relief and say, "Thank goodness I can change this!" We now look upon change as normal, and for the purposes of evolution, maturity, growth of prosperity, and steps toward enlightenment.

Does the phrase **change is hard** then block or discourage us from achieving positive changes? Cultural changes, even the no brainers, are indeed difficult to implement. For goodness sakes, women were ridiculed, beaten, and arrested during the suffragette movement. The resistance to allowing women the privilege of their votes was intense and formidable--what on Earth could that lead to? What if females began to expect equality in other areas? What a disastrous outcome that would be! But I must acknowledge that the men in power during the British Suffragette Movement did indeed find it in their hearts to enact some positive change--the Cat and Mouse Act of 1913. Well done! And finally, most incarcerated women gone wild were released. But **all's fair in love and war**: it had been determined that these subjugated citizens were much more helpful to the war effort when they were outside of prison and working, rather than when these girls behaving badly were starving in jail.

All sarcasm aside, is change really hard? It can be. But do humans cling to the statement as an excuse to dig their heels in? Massive changes seem to spring up quite spontaneously, such as the implemen- tation of the Gregorian calendar. And yet so many sensible and help- ful advancements languish in the hearts and minds of governments, communities, and individuals everywhere such as the Harkin–Engel Protocol. This international call to action compels chocolate suppliers to stop using children as slaves on cacao plantations. Yet, according to the Protocol, these corporations have 10 years to comply. I guess **change is hard**.

It is common knowledge that humans base their behaviors and ex- pectation largely on previous occurrences. **That's just the way things are**, and other equally disempowering mantras have convinced many of us to resist change. But when we break down the types of change we encounter along our journeys through life, we understand that we are only *making* change hard where it is not necessarily so. We constantly repeat the phrase, **change is hard**, out loud, to ourselves and each other. It's like reminding everybody that we're screwed! This mental construct, applied to the ever-changing process of humanity, serves no one. Let us alter our perception of change and see how experience now becomes new and improved. Don't brace yourself, rather embrace the winds of change which carry fresh outlooks, second chances, creative ideas, and choices. Let the power of the Mayan White Wind imbue your soul with the spirit of understanding, advancement, and freedom.

Chapter 13

The More Things Change the More They Stay the Same

Wow! Everybody's saying it, in one form or another. From the Old Testament book of Ecclesiastes, to contemporary rock star Pete Townshend, to futurists Jose Arguelles and Stephanie South. But is this true? And is it uttered in a spirit of despair? Or is it a knowing--an understanding of the cycle of creation? The examples I just noted are all indicative of the understanding that this manipulation, or a version of it, actually depicts the reality of life on Earth. But, these artists and perhaps you and I, all have dramatically differing opinions of what this statement truly means. Further, our differing viewpoints about the nature and reality of change can lead to vastly different life experiences. As we examine this, and other weird sayings about change as "not really change", we may want to review our own perspectives! **Easier said than done**?

The more things change the more they stay the same is indeed accurate, but deceptive in the way we process it as a third, or even fourth dimensional thought form. In its expression today, this statement is a lament. The songwriter referenced earlier, and the appearance of the title phrase of this chapter, all present as misguided confirmation that we live in a continuous loop of undesired life experiences.

Here is that understanding, expressed in the form of a brilliant musical piece entitled Won't get Fooled Again, by The Who. Just a small excerpt is all we need in order to hear, nod in agreement, and accept.

There's nothing in the streets
Looks any different to me
And the slogans are replaced, by the bye
And a parting on the left
Is now a parting on the right
And the beards have all grown longer overnight

The cyclical theories of involution and evolution are explained in *Book of the Throne*, by Jose Arguelles and Stephanie South. One need only advance into the first chapter to see that all creation of matter occurs as a manifestation of thought forms of the soul. Thus, the perceived reality of creation is a result of soul purpose, and once the thought form has evolved to that state, the involution activity begins again.

Within the understanding of the sixth dimensional laws of matter as creations of the soul, we now realize our true power as humans. Do those humans who are currently running the show understand this? Do they purposely repeat disempowering phrases such as this to keep us from trying to effect personalized outcomes? I doubt it. Instead, it is entirely possible that we have become lazy in our acceptance of the status quo--is that all there is? Or, has this become such a widely accepted belief that we, ironically, continue to live it out over and over again?

Consider for a moment that Pete Townshend, when he wrote "Won't Get Fooled Again", did understand the expanded perspectives we see in *Book of the Throne*. Was he simply mocking the propensity of humans to keep running in the hamster wheel, without realizing the infinite opportunities for change which lie all around and within? I hope they haven't gotten to him, too!

Scripturally, we see the theory of **the more things change the more they stay the same** in action. But examine the upcoming verse with focused attention. Look at it now with a fresh perspective, and a more open mind. Meditate on it, pray on it, dream about the possibilities.

"The thing that hath been, it is that which shall be; and that which is done is that which shall be done: and there is no new thing under the sun." (Ecclesiastes 1:9 KJVA).

Does this refer to the *process*, and the same pattern of manifestation as written in the Arguelles/South texts? The *cycle* is that which is not new. The *outcomes*, however, are ever changing and ever-evolving. This is a different way to look at it, as if with head askance. King Solomon is credited by many bible scholars as the author of Ecclesiastes. He is also credited as having powerful wisdom endowed upon him, at his request, by God. To me, the commonly accepted, lowly definition of this citation is not indicative of something which would come from a man who is timelessly revered as espousing divine wisdom. We are missing something.

The interesting part of my own ramblings here is a look back at the opening paragraph. This phrase has come forward from ancient beginnings to future evolutive stages. Will it come full circle? Is that what's really meant by this interesting philosophy? Further, could this be what we perhaps instinctively know when we say: "**Everything that goes around comes around**"? Again, we surely cannot be dumbing that last one down to a simple warning: **karma's a bitch**!

PART 4

THE INNER CHILD

"After all these came also the little children, those who pos-sess the knowledge of the father. When they became strong they were taught the aspects of the father's face. They came to know and they were known. They were glorified and they gave glory." (The Gospel of Truth).

One of my favorite things to do: channel the remarkable Carl Jung. Dr. Carl Jung (1875-1961) was a Swiss psychiatrist. His exquisite work greatly advanced the practices of psychology and therapy. Among all Jung's work, his theories on archetypes is most fascinating for me.

The Child is a Jungian Archetype, and it plays an important role in the individuation process--another of Jung's profound discoveries. This archetype may represent an undeveloped part of a human per-sonality, and it also represents potentialities and future developments. According to Jung, the archetype of The Child is a part of each of us. Variations and additional descriptors accompany the child archetype.

One such is the Child Hero--and who better to exemplify this than the Ascended Master, Jesus.

In a beautifully crafted text, Kaia Ra records her channeled messages from the Ascended Master Quan Yin. In her book *The Sophia Code*, Kaia Ra reveals the forgotten teachings of karuna, or mercy and compassion. The author then goes on to describe karuna for self, as a deeply loving, maternal gift of nurturing. The message from Quan Yin, through Kaia Ra, is that by extending this level of karuna to ourselves, we can begin to parent our own Inner Child, as part of a journey toward complete healing and wholeness.

Come with me now into the Secret Garden. These two words, secret and garden, when paired, describe a children's book, movies, songs, and even a South Korean television series. The Secret Garden is a metaphor. It may represent that which is forgotten, untended, lost, or shameful. The Secret Garden is the world of hidden potentials--beauty, nature, growth, and life. The Secret Garden, to me, is the Inner Child--innocent, curious, natural, and uncorrupted. But why is our childlike part of us sometimes referred to as secret? Jung certainly did not label it as such. Is it supposed to be concealed? Are we taught, just by the pairing of the two words, secret and garden, that it should be forgotten, ignored, or perhaps **seen but not heard**? What have we done with that pure part of us--the joyous and the excitable part? Why are we secreting this most precious child?

Many of us have forgotten how to play. We stopped climbing trees. No longer do we lie on the floor with an open coloring book, and crayons rolling around. Some adults still do these things, and they retain their childlike view of the world: an enormous playground. But some have left that life behind. Perhaps we stop exploring, learning, and playing because we have been told to stop. But what if it never occurred to us to delineate childhood and adulthood as so vastly different? Are we not the same person, at any age--with the same soul and the same personality? Instead of looking at childhood and adulthood as completely separate, find the overlap. By merging the archetypes and the growth stages, we continue to be a whole person.

By looking at the progression of life as one distinct and separate stage from the previous, we quite possibly fragment ourselves.

Instead, I call for a remembrance of the joys of childhood--the running, the jumping, the exploring, and the climbing. Writing this section really made me think about climbing trees and how much I missed that. I closed my eyes and imagined myself going back to a large tree in my grandmother's yard. My brother, cousins, and I would always climb it and just hang out in the branches, talking our kid nonsense from one to another. I smiled thinking how some of us would struggle to keep up, hanging on while trying to swing a leg over each branch. None of us cared how we looked in the process, the mission was simply to get there. In fact, being the only one on the ground while everyone else was in the tree was a fate nobody was having, no matter how foolish we looked scrambling up there. What an interesting memory to come into play at this time in my life. Do you remember? I do.

Speaking of coloring, didn't you always have a favorite color? I did. Is this connected to the 12 Rays of Light?

And did you ever watch an ant and wonder if we, also, were as a tiny ant on a speck called Earth? And that an immense universe was out there, waiting to be discovered?

I am still that child. You are as well. And, in our wisdom and maturity, we can now learn more, access more, make our own decisions, and create our own realities on this planet--our great, big playground. Remember: when it was time to go out and play, we just went out. Our neighbors were our friends. We chose our games through groupthink process. We instinctively identified personality types of our peers. We left the group to retreat to solitary play when we desired it. All of these things were natural, unspoken, and mostly unconscious.

Now we take classes to identify our own personality type. Don't we already know ourselves? We often don't associate with our physical neighbors even though we most likely chose to live we were do. Do we enter into meetings at work, fully expecting that a decision will made, and the games will begin? Perhaps we have turned away from ourselves as natural children and have, instead, become quite unnatural adults.

The following pages in this section will describe the lies we tell children. Jesus taught Truth to his newbie followers. Those who followed him listened of their own free will and discerned for themselves what to believe. Jesus led through the use of parables. Children do not always want to hear what we want to tell them. They have not always come willingly. Most parents and teachers have experienced a child who tunes out. The wonderful work of Charles Schultz and his Peanut Gang illustrates just how oblivious kids can be. Within the animated short films, we hear the voices of the invisible adults and their "wauh, wauh, wauh", and realize that children do not speak the same language. So instead, adults must cleverly find a way to get the message across.

The lies we tell children are taught through games, nursery rhymes and animal metaphors. Because, God forbid these little darlings have an incorrect understanding of humanity. Sooner or later they must grow up--can't be kids forever! The rug must be pulled out from under them, the bubbles must burst, and they simply must learn "reality". The methodologies, most especially the apologues concealed within popular fairy tales, are developed to ensure that these little innocents will learn just how crappy life is. That, my children, is the mother of all lies.

Chapter 14

You Can't Have Your Cake and Eat it Too

What the heck? Seriously? What does that even mean? Holy macaroni where do humans come up with these things? I'd really like to tell you how we came up with that one, but at this point the origin is completely moot. It's an even dumber way of saying **"you can't have it all"**, or **"you can't have the best of both worlds"**. **You can't have your cake and eat it too** is defended by comments suggesting that desiring two mutually exclusive rewards is unreasonable. Again, what? So, if you eat your cake you no longer have it? Okay. I get that. But why on earth would I want to have a cake if I wasn't going to eat it? Oh, "have" means "eat", you say—like: "Let's have lunch." Outwardly this may appear as a grammatically weird statement, and nothing more. But what if it truly is a way to blatantly place limitations on what we can acquire for ourselves? Who gets to do this? Trust me on this one.

Imagine your birthday--say, when you were turning 10, and your parents presented you with a cake and candles. They sang to you and encouraged you to make a wish and blow out the candles. Everyone clapped, and celebrated you, and gave their gifts of love to you. Did the party then stop? Tell me what happened next. Think hard. Did everyone sigh and look wistfully at the cake and declare: you have your cake, but you can't eat it? I doubt that very much. Yes, my literal depiction is ridiculous, but is it? You can tell me now that the phrase is a metaphor, and not to be taken literally. I'm still not convinced.

Let's dig down into what folks really mean when they say **you can't have your cake and eat it too**. The purpose is quite clear--to place limitations upon the potentials of another. That's it. There's no other reason to use this phrase. For starters, it imposes restrictions on how self-entitled we should feel. That "entitlement" word makes us all squirm a little, for a variety of reasons. Entitlement is closely associated with narcissism, and that's a badge nobody really wants to wear. Unless of course you really are a narcissist-- in that case you don't care. But self-entitlement is a little different, and I want to look at it in a different way--my way! Typically, entitled people are defined as those who believe they should have more than others--they believe they are more valuable and deserve more. Sometimes these people are referred to using a word I won't repeat (starts with an A and everyone's got one). But now I want to redefine self-entitlement. What if we each believed that we were valuable enough to legitimately expect a constant influx of cake into our lives, and not at anyone else's expense? We could even go so far as to agree that everyone is of that same understanding, and each is entitled to the same quality of life--joyful, loving, and abundant. Why not? In today's world, there is more than enough. Tons of food are wasted from supermarkets and restaurants every day. People are denied medications because they can't afford them, while the pharmaceutical companies make bank. Those are just a couple of examples of the plenteous resources that all people should be able to enjoy. So why are we made to feel greedy, or guilty, or unworthy because we **want to have our cake and eat it too**?

The idea that accomplishments **can only go so far** is factual and practical to many, many people. To others, this notion is preposterous. Where does your journey stop? When does it cap off? When have we gone too far, and who gets to decide? We see so many people who have accomplished seemingly miraculous things. They have conquered great difficulties, overcome the odds, and risen to success through nearly impossible circumstances. We often learn about these people and feel overwhelming admiration, and, oftentimes, a wistful resignation that they are the exception. Perhaps they are, but perhaps they don't need to be. I say this not to diminish the achievements of those who have worked so hard, but rather to say that these examples should demonstrate that which all of us can do. People who have beaten the odds are living examples of why we should not impose any type of limitations on others. Does it not further honor these people when we actually learn to apply their mentality to our everyday lives? Perhaps their purpose lies there--not in their personal achievement(s) alone but in their gift of embodying the potentials of every human, as example for all.

This dumb phrase, **you can't have your cake and eat it too,** does not call for a long, drawn out chapter. Rather I will get off of this rant shortly, but one more thing: there are lots and lots of people who enjoy fabulous success, have lots of cake, and they eat it whenever they want to. What is different for them? Attitude. As a fan and follower of Abraham-Hicks and their team's work, I have learned, and experienced, that attitude is everything.

The work of Esther and Jerry Hicks, along with the channeled messages of Abraham, has changed lives all over the planet. Their extensive collection of books, including *Ask and it is Given*, will teach you how to make choices for yourself that bring happiness, prosperity, and all the cake you can eat. This organization appears, at least to me, to be the leading expert on leveraging the universal laws of attraction and vibration. Their work will certainly make a believer out of you! My advice: Get the book and read it too.

Chapter 15

Curiosity Killed the Cat

What does this mean? It is a warning! Danger lies ahead, and dire consequences. Whatever it is that you are seeking to explore will harm you, or bite you, or possibly even kill you! Wow, what a scary world! Could it be true that a desire to learn about, or understand something will somehow place us in grave peril?

Why would someone discourage another from being inquisitive, interested, and hungry for understanding? Is it simply a tool to protect children from their own naivete? Or could the intention behind the adage be more sinister than it first appears?

This distortion--**curiosity killed the cat**--suggests that we should intentionally hinder ourselves from gaining knowledge. Further, we are instructed to remain in a state of compliance or acceptance of the status quo. This is powerfully connected to other manipulations brought to light within this book: especially the adage **don't rock the boat**. Is this a classic case of overthinking? Hear me out, and then decide for yourself.

Mizaru, Kikazaru, and Iwazaru are the sagacious monkeys which are found carved into the Tōshō-gū shrine located in Nikkō, Japan. The sculptor was Hidari Jingoro, and it is believed that he sought to reflect a tenet of Confucius. And modern society still refers to the monkeys with the following, similar interpretation: hear no evil, speak no evil, see no evil. Today we learn about hundreds of possible nuances associated with Jingoro's ancient art. Do the monkeys tell us to avoid all that is evil? Is the carved panel meant to warn us? Or is it part of a systemic call to blind humans from truth?

The assumedly well-intended philosophy of Confucius is loosely in keeping with some biblical principles meant to teach us to remove ourselves from anything corruptive. And before we get into the precise scriptural references, consider that the combined books of Job, Ecclesiastes, and Proverbs are considered the three "Wisdom Books". Is it a stretch to notice: three wisdom books of the Catholic Bible and three wise monkeys? Coincidence?

The letters of Saint Paul, and some brilliant responses from Jesus, demonstrate the connection between what goes in to us, and what comes out of us. "O generation of vipers, how can ye, being evil, speak good things? for out of the abundance of the heart the mouth speaketh." (Matthew 12:34 KJVA). And, Proverbs is all about avoiding foolish behaviors--no monkeying around here!

> "My son, hear the instruction of thy father, and forsake not the law of thy mother:" (Proverbs 1:8 KJVA).

> "My son, let not them depart from thine eyes: keep sound wisdom and discretion:" (Proverbs 3:21 KJVA).

> "Hear, O my son, and receive my sayings; and the years of thy life shall be many." (Proverbs 4:10 KJVA).

> "Let no corrupt communication proceed out of your mouth, but that which is good to the use of edifying, that it may minister grace unto the hearers." (Ephesians 4:29 KJVA).

But how do we determine what is corrupt and what is not? How does one discern? Is that not the operative word here--discernment?

Learning is a process--a journey. We must be curious. We must investigate. How can there be discernment with the absence of exploring complexities, questioning processes, and critically evaluating our world? How do we learn? Where is the development to come from, and how do we grow?

Enough with the monkeys for now.

As my readers undoubtedly expect, I must now bring to notice the practice of assigning sinful, and even deadly curiosity as a practice among women. From Genesis, we learn that Eve, the only female in existence, disobeyed God. She was tempted, as the story goes, and was beguiled by a more cunning creature than herself--a snake. For those who are believers in literal interpretation, we see a talking snake (with a forked tongue) who, with a brain only fraction in size of a human brain, was exceedingly more clever than this adult human, Eve. She was tricked into disobedience because she was seduced by not only the beauty of the fruit, but by the very thirst for knowledge we all possess from birth. Because of Eve's desire for gnosis, she has forever invoked a great curse upon all of humanity--forever meaning forever--you know, for all of eternity.

Compare this now to the concept of bluebearding, which is based upon an ancient legend about a powerful and wealthy man. Bluebeard possessed riches beyond measure, yet he could not find a loving wife. Each time he married, his current wife was put to the test--she may enter any room of the castle and enjoy any and all freedoms and pleasures that were available, as long as she followed one simple rule: she was forbidden to unlock and peer into the secret chamber. In succession, each wife would succumb to her curiosity, and discover the gruesome corpses of the previous wives--each having met her demise through uxoricide. Because of an uncontrollable urge to discover, and thus a willingness to disobey, each Mrs. Bluebeard provided her husband with justification for murder. Some would say she had it coming!

Curiosity is a natural inclination, and a healthy way to explore everything--from our own bodies to what lies beyond the cosmos. A state of curiosity feels like a return to our Inner Child, and a return to that feeling of wonder. Humans have instinctive desires to ask, to connect, and to search for truth. This is an amazing universe we live in, and it contains infinite mysteries. The suppression of curiosity is an act of denying ourselves.

But let us not forget that the word "curiosity" is a noun. And other definitions of it include odd or interesting items, or puzzling things. Is it possible that this phrase originated because somebody's cat was killed by a falling knick knack? Perhaps the frisky feline destroyed a cherished heirloom, or perhaps a curious child did some damage and blamed the cat. Anyway, my ridiculous theories are all intended to prove one thing: discouraging a human's natural tendency to be curious is absurd at best, and, at worst, nefarious.

Peer closer now, don't be afraid! What does all of this mean? Who was Confucius? Didn't Jesus say: "' For every one that asketh receiveth; and he that seeketh findeth; and to him that knocketh it shall be opened ?' (Luke 11:10,KJV). What is hidden from us, and why? What is the meaning of life?--aren't you just *dying* to know?

Chapter 16

Don't Get Your Hopes Up

You may say I'm a dreamer
But I'm not the only one
I hope some day you'll join us
*And the world will be as one...*John Lennon

I imagine Mr. Lennon was a dreamer from very early on. I wonder if he possessed a spirit of time and space travel, as he envisioned a world full of love and abundance. As a child, did he imagine tremendous accomplishments and fantastical journeys through life? Were his visions always lofty, idealistic, and epic? What he did know for sure: he is not the only one. So many of us, especially children, dare to dream big.

Let me tell you a story of a little girl with dreams as big as John Lennon's. She had visions of peace, love, and the end of poverty. She dreamed of a world without suffering. And oftentimes this innocent soul would enthusiastically bubble over and describe her visions to anyone who would listen. This child's mother would hear the rantings of a hopeless little dreamer, and would, predictably, respond with a ditty. It was a funny little song about an ant and a rubber tree plant. Mother would quietly sing a portion of the song, which served to painfully warn the little girl that dreams of such magnitude, and of such great and beautiful accomplishments, were folly. For those of you who haven't yet realized: the song to which I refer was written in 1959 by Jimmy Van Heusen and Sammy Cahn and was performed most notably by Frank Sinatra. The song was later awarded an Oscar and has been sung by other such great vocal artists as Sammy Davis, Jr. and Bing Crosby. This song is entitled "High Hopes" and the lyrics describe an ambitious little ant who perseveres through a project which appears impossible--moving a rubber tree plant. The song, although not the original version, was even used in 1960 as the theme song for the John F. Kennedy presidential campaign.

But did a young and impressionable child truly understand the meaning behind the song? Without ever learning the remaining lyrics to the song and having never been told the spirit behind the response, this little one grew up believing that she faced impossible odds, and she believed failure was a certainty--all because the design of the song "High Hopes" remained a mystery to her. Whether intended or not, the message of this repetitious action became a catalyst for sadness, hopelessness, and defeat.

But did you know that an ant can move items of great proportion according to its own weight? Depending on who we listen to, scientists tell us that ants can hold weight which exceeds anywhere from 100 to 1,000 times their own weight. Herein lies the irony of the hopes and dreams of billions of souls being compared to an ant and a tree. "High Hopes" is meant to rouse people, and to encourage dreamers not to wake up. Know this: the ant who plays the starring role in this ditty finally accomplishes his stupendous feat of moving the plant.

It is understandable that people use the motto **don't get your hopes up** with a pure intent: to protect a loved one from possible disappointment. But in doing so, are the ones who deliver this warning projecting their own fears onto others? For so many, hope is a catalyst for positive action, and hope illuminates the path toward purpose. And for so many, hope is the very thread of survival to which a suffering soul may cling. Who, then, could dash the hopes of one who may hang on tightly to a lofty hope as their only way to believe in a better world? Would you snuff out a light, at the end of someone's tunnel? Perhaps not intentionally.

In my first book, *Pray Without Ceasing*, I ask my readers to feel the omnipotent power of hope. The message is to watch what we say to each other. And now I repeat some of the painful terminology about hope--less subtle yet every bit as destructive as "**don't get your hopes up**":

"It is hopeless"

"All hope is lost"

"I hope things get better"

So, which is it? Do we hope or not? Do we not arm ourselves with posters, screensavers, and affirmations reminding us to never give up? Are we disempowering ourselves through the act of hope? Or are we disempowering ourselves through the act of rejecting hope? Does this conundrum not represent the paradox of humanity? Make up your mind already!

Did Kennedy win the 1960 election? He most certainly did, and as the youngest president elect in history, and the first Catholic president, one might venture to say that John F. Kennedy is the ant that moved the rubber tree plant. So, let us strike this phrase from our list of clichés, and let us instead courageously inspire each other to hope, to dream, and to believe.

Let us be as the ranks of the ants. They march on, in militant defiance of all discouraging remarks and disheartening attitudes from humans. They smugly join forces and move rubber trees all over the world. The fall of Apartheid and the demolition of the Berlin Wall represent the most ominous of rubber trees. Yet humanity continued to hope and believe that peace could come. I still hope that you will join us, the dreamers. John and I are waiting.

Chapter 17

Finders Keepers

When I was a kid my family would watch the evening news during dinner, on a little television set in the kitchen. Generally, the news was disturbing to me, and I always tried to tune it out. But one night an interesting report caught my attention. An armored car had crashed somewhere, and money had spilled out. The reporter announced that there had been a traffic jam and a mad rush, as people grabbed handfuls of paper money and dashed off. There I was in my innocence, with a forkful of mashed potatoes midair, eyes wide, body frozen in time. I remember asking my parents: "Isn't that stealing?"

A distant voice was heard cutting through my momentary brain fog, and it said: "**Finders keepers**". I'm not sure who said it--whether it was a family member or somebody on the news network. I'm not really sure if anybody even said it at all. But, at that moment, those two words were very present for me, and forever changed the way I looked at nursery rhymes, fairy tales, weird phrases, and the evening news.

Here's an amusing side note: we all know by now that the childhood game of Ring a Ring O' Roses is possibly all about dropping dead from The Plague, right? That was a gruesome discovery for me as well.

My point is, why are we keeping these slogans alive? Are we still teaching them to our children? Are our parents teaching them to our children? Most likely, yes, somebody is.

Back to the **finders keepers** mess. Isn't this a subtle justification for stealing? Perhaps some confusion has caused us to forget the origins of this phrase. Some other common verses are also connected to this one:

1. **"One man's loss is another man's gain"**. This is powerfully resonant of the "**finders keepers**" rhyme. By losing something of value, another now will benefit. Can gain occur without the experience of loss? This could be deeper than we realize at first glance. The Death card, in the Tarot, tells us of the ending of an old paradigm and the rebirth of it into something new. This saying about "gain" is also in keeping with New Age theories about death as a metaphor for something which no longer serves the higher purpose of the human. And, even the bible tells us that a seed must die before it can manifest into a new life. Where am I going with all this death stuff--am I off track? What I am getting to is this: what if the "one man" and the "another man", in the above mentioned phrase, are really one and the same! Perhaps we can now see the story of loss and gain, finders and keepers, as a metaphor for transformation, growth, renewal, and progress? What if somebody mixed that up from way back when, and this children's idiom was not meant to be an excuse for thievery, but instead it is an expression of a natural cycle of loss and gain?

2. "One man's trash is another man's treasure". This one is not nearly as deep, or as interesting. Since there's no accounting for taste, someone may be repulsed by an object, or person, while someone else is attracted to it and desires to possess it. This phrase is not quite aligned with the **finders keepers** one, but in doing some research I discovered that many people oftentimes carelessly confuse the two and consider them as the same.

Now you see why I had called all of this a mess. Did we clean it up? Probably not. But this manipulation is important in the sense that it reminds us to watch our step. How easy it is to fail to observe our own behaviors, and sometimes fall into less than ethical decisions. This phrase teaches children exactly what I fear.

I will concede that this rhyme is often used as a way for parents to warn children that they must keep their belongings about them, and not misplace them. But are we really keeping watch over our stuff because we want to continue possessing it, or do we now guard our property with an air of mistrust and suspicion? What, really, are we teaching? Are we teaching that if we lose something, we should *expect* it to be returned to us? Or do we *expect* that whoever finds it will keep it? And, how important is *expectation*? Some say that expectation is the deciding factor of the outcome of our lives. I guess that calls for another book!

In my true Pollyanna style, I ask that we please stop saying this rhyme. Stop saying it, stop teaching it, stop expecting it, and for goodness sakes please don't ever live it!

Chapter 18

Be Careful What You Wish For

"Oh deary dear". Willie Wonka.

Of course, when we think about wishes, we immediately think about Aladdin, the protagonist, in *One Thousand and One Nights*, by Antoine Galland. And there's another childhood wish association in the Disney movie, *Pinocchio*. The beloved Jiminy Cricket encourages all to "wish upon a star". We make a wish before we blow out our birthday candles. I could go on and on about the millions of associations with the *act* of wishing that we learn from early childhood. Let me rephrase that last remark, and from now on let us call it the *art* of wishing.

Intention is an art form. Intending is an advanced form of wishing. When one approaches something with intent, one has already determined the outcome. Good. Solid. Known. But when one wishes for something, it's a hopeful way of wanting something while at the same time believing there is little likelihood of receiving it. Not good. Sad. Bummer. Is it that way for you? Check this out:

Intending is saying: "I'm going to get that!" Or, "I'm going to do that!"

Wishing is saying: "I want that but won't get it". Or, "I want to do that, but I can't." Wishing is all about having a big but!

Humanity has developed an overwhelming number of words and nuances within our world's languages in order to use language to create conditioning. This entire book is about the importance of precise language. And sometimes this becomes a little bit of an obsession for me, but it's important. And now I have a song stuck in my head! And I'm all about the 80's! In 1983, The Fixx released an interesting song entitled: "One Thing Leads to Another". I thought of this song while pondering my frustration over careless communication. On that note, perhaps we should not only stop saying **be careful what you wish for**, we might consider declaring a moratorium on the word "wishing" until we figure this out.

Tell me now, what you really believe. What is in your heart of hearts? Do we all secretly know that words contain powers of creation? Maybe we should just admit it: what we say happens! What you speak about, you bring about. Let's get this on the table and put it right out front. And while we're talking about "outing" our beliefs that we speak things into happening let us now talk about all the different ways we do so.

Magick. Once again, we see linguistic nuances intended to both clarify and confuse. Many people only refer to this topic as it relates to magic: the practice of tricking others. Magick is something completely different. The history of human powers of creation go back thousands of years and can be learned from very early recorded history. Yet, somewhere along the line, manifestation through words became a demonized art. As recently as the 18th Century A.D., women have been executed for witchcraft. Sacred healing arts through nature's botanical kingdom was also outlawed. This perspective was so wildly erroneous, it is like shooting yourself in the foot.

Spells. These are well-defined intentions. Even the word "spell" has a complex definition. Spelling is defined as an arrangement of letters. Precise communication occurs when the letters are arranged correctly. A spell is defined as an arrangement of words. Manifestation occurs according to the correct arrangement of the words in the spell. But, once again, there is history of oppression. Somehow, speaking intention into being was labelled as "black magic", and something to be feared. Herein is the evidence that speaking is creating.

Curses. These only work if the cursee believes it has power. It then becomes their own belief that manifests. That's just what I think. Contact me if you want to discuss this. I'm serious. To me, a curse is just a dirty word that comes out of someone's mouth.

Prayer. The power of words is everywhere in our religious beliefs. Prayers are supposed to be requests to God. We ask for what we want. We cry out, we plead for intercession, and we worship through prayer. We expect that He hears all.

God spoke creation of the world, and of Jesus. "And the Word was made flesh, and dwelt among us, (and we beheld his glory, the glory as of the only begotten of the Father,) full of grace and truth." (John 1:14 KJVA).

Jesus told us to ask for whatever we want. "Ask, and it shall be given you; seek, and ye shall find; knock, and it shall be opened unto you." (Matthew 7:7 KJVA).

Here's another call to action, from Saint James: "Ye lust, and have not: ye kill, and desire to have, and cannot obtain: ye fight and war, yet ye have not, because ye ask not." (James 4:2 KJVA).

Do we say **"be careful what you wish for"** as a warning because we know the power contained within our spoken word? Yet, if I say I am intending something into reality, then I become the subject of laughter, and ridicule. Is the concept of speaking manifestations so farfetched? Then why the warning? See the circular reasoning/argument here? At the end of the day, if people didn't believe words have power, then we would not have this warning: **"Be careful what you wish for"**.

To continue with the opening quote in this chapter, I conclude with this one, also stated by the beloved Gene Wilder in his unforgettable role as Willy Wonka: "Don't forget what happened to the man who suddenly got everything he always wanted."

Chapter 19

Sticks and Stones

Another example of paradox! What are we teaching our children? This is a classic example of talking out of both sides of our mouths, and here's why:

1. Those in the know wish to impart that it doesn't matter what anyone else thinks of you. I have a close friend who reminds me that "it's none of your business what someone else thinks about you". Yes, she's right (as usual). Many strive to accept and understand that others are lashing out when they speak harshly. Often, the out of control person is not even thinking about the poor soul on the receiving end of their verbal attack. Rather, their own pain or inner turmoil is their primary driver. The nearest human may simply represent the nearest target. I applaud the parents who try to teach this principle, however many children do not yet possess the emotion intelligence, maturity, or wisdom to comprehend this concept. After all--how many adults do you know that haven't figured this out yet?

2. We don't want to be raising a teaser, do we? Don't we teach children that its mean and hurtful to call each other names? Yet when a wounded spirit reports some verbal abuse, we turn

around and try to convince them it doesn't hurt--that their pain is imagined, or not legitimate. Talk about adding insult to injury. What we are saying is: it is wrong for you to do it, and it is wrong to be hurt when someone does it to you. How does that make any sense?

3. The bottom line is this: by singing that little "sticks and stones" song, aren't we just weaseling out of dealing with a bully? It certainly would be a lot easier to brainwash the victim into accepting what's happened. We do it all the time. It's quite disruptive when someone is called on the carpet for bad behavior. So, we keep accepting it. After all, we need to get along to go along, right? But what if we began to stand up for ourselves? What if there were a new sheriff in town? Imagine the implications--people could even start an entire movement against sweeping bad behavior under the carpet! But that won't ever happen. It's much easier to go with the flow, let it roll off, and move on. The tormentor gets a pass, and the offense is dismissed as not valid. The haters keep hating, and everyone just keeps sucking it up. Do you find yourself falling into this trap? #metoo!

Yes, the three points above left us with an unanswered question: Why? Why are we perpetuating this disempowering invention? The truth is, sticks and stones most certainly do break our bones. But words are weapons of psychological and emotional devastation. Words can be permanently destructive. They cut to our very souls and create wounds which, although mostly invisible, can fester and disempower us--sometimes for a lifetime. And who doesn't appreciate a good proverb to fall back on when we forget how important our words actually are. "Death and life are in the power of the tongue…" (Proverbs 18:21 KJVA). I choose life.

PART 5

RELATIONSHIPS

Lies can have a profound impact on relationships. As each of us strives to live in truth, so must be the standard for a relationship. Otherwise there is an unbalanced experience, and perhaps a floundering or a faltering of the union, whatever type it may be.

The essays within this upcoming section are all connected to relationships. The topics range from the dynamics of intimate relationships, to taking our "place" in society. What we do, or what we believe, determines the outcomes of our lives according to our alignment with our purposes. Simply put, untruths derail human lives. So why do some of us live in this state--misaligned with what, for each of us, is our Truth? I have a theory: conditioning. This single descriptor, which you see many times within my work, is the method for keeping us in the dark. When children learn falsehoods about the nature of humanity and lies about the reality of who they are as individuals, they become conditioned. And, when unexamined, they go on to condition others, namely their own offspring, in much the same manner. This, quite possibly could be the "unexamined life" that Socrates is believed to have commented on. Critical thinking has become somewhat of a lost art, and one which supposedly lies beneath Socrates' notion to question authority. And, although we all still quote Socrates all day long, do we really practice what we preach?

Hang in there with me, as I further assert that conditioning can lead us in two directions. There will always be middle ground, shades of grey, and outliers, but here are the two distant points, upon my imagined spectrum of results, that emerge from exposure to serious and artificial social conditioning.

Apathy. We are oblivious, or don't care. People get lazy. I annoy people with my ideas, and they shake their heads, throw up their hands, and tell me to cut it out. What is that? Perhaps it's just too much to process. Yet I continue to press: doesn't anybody care? Isn't anybody listening? Is real, or so-called active listening another lost art? (And I've just given you two hints in this essay about another upcoming book so get excited please!)

After watching movies like *The Matrix* and *Invasion of the Body Snatchers*, along with reading books like George Orwell's brilliant work, published in 1949, entitled *1984*, I wonder if this isn't already happening. People sometimes come off as robotic, emotionless, and just going through the motions. Apathy is dangerous as it can lead to acceptance of things that, upon examination, are quite unacceptable. For example, think about the issue of desensitization--there are many professional theories that support this somewhat terrifying concept. Repeated exposure to simulated violence, leading to desensitization, is what I fear the most.

Control. This is where we swim into shark-infested waters. Some intentionally seek power or control over others. And the control freaks of the world are often willing to go to extremes in order to get what they are after. Manipulation is really a thing, and it can range from overt to subtle to invisible. Think gaslighting. Is rage fueling the urge to control? Where does that type of destructive energy come from? Without getting too weird, I venture to say that, as mentioned above, imbalance has come into play here. Has conditioning led to disconnection from self or Source, which has led to rage, which now leads to seriously controlling behavior? The stories in the news about domestic violence, and the intimate partner murder rate is beyond alarming. It may be a huge stretch, for some, to connect this type of dysfunction with lies, but I stand behind my belief that living outside of our truth is unnatural at best. In so many cases, living a lie is devastating.

Where is a remedy? Is there relief? Can this all be out of whack, and just interesting conversation? Sometimes the truth hides and is corrupted or concealed by untruths. But at other times, truth is right there, laying out in the open, right under our noses. We need only wake up and open our eyes to the possibilities that surround us. The depth of who we are is infinite, the journey to understanding is endless, and the experience of discovery is at once shocking, perhaps, but then joyful. Come with me, hang out, let's and celebrate truth!

Chapter 20

Everything Happens for a Reason

This is an interesting phrase, and it is somewhat controversial. I wasn't even sure what my position was on this one, so I listened to others. There appear to be good arguments for both sides of this notion, and whether it is true or false. Therefore, I approach this chapter by talking out of both sides of my mouth.

The Two Dimensions of Reason are the contrasting perspectives of 3D thinking patterns versus Higher Dimensional thinking patterns:

1. *Third, or purely physical, dimensional viewpoint.* I think my biggest point of contention is when people use "**everything happens for a reason**" to justify a tragedy to those who are most impacted by it. Well intentioned people actually offer this message thinking it will provide comfort. We are forced to accept that no matter what happens, there must be a really good reason out there that we'll just never know. As my saucy cousin would say: "*Innnnnteresting....*" Perhaps if enough people believe this explanation, then it will, in actuality, become its own self-fulfilling prophecy. Thus, people will just have to learn to accept that tragedy is random and

occurs under unknown conditions. Perhaps this phenomenon is true, or perhaps it limits the human mind from taking a higher perspective.

When a parent loses a child through death, I often hear outsiders inform the grieving family that "God needed another angel", or some similarly unhelpful words. These types of responses demonstrate a lack of understanding about the true nature of why things happen. I'm not going to claim here that I, and I alone, understand the concepts behind the Supreme Creative Intelligence of our world, because that would be arrogant. But it is also, in my humble opinion, arrogant to assume that some well-connected folks know the intentions and actions of God--that He, seemingly randomly, decides to strike a child with diabetes, or crush a group of men within a mine, or make Wall Street crash. I do not wish to offend those who ascribe to this philosophy-- I did add "In my humble opinion", so that makes it okay.

What about the incidences when we use "**everything happens for a reason**" as an excuse? We mess up, the fallout is disastrous, we shrug, and we cover ourselves with this manipulation. This strategy is intended to not only insincerely beg forgiveness for an oversight but may actually succeed to translate the error into a service. Depends how good you are.

2. *Other, or innate, dimensional viewpoint.* Tom Kenyon is a channel, and he provides fascinating information in his book *The Hathor Material.* In the book, concepts of Absolute and Relative Realms of Consciousness are briefly introduced. This teaching speaks of the relationship between all phenomena, including that which occurs as sensory experience. So, in an expansive mentality, we would understand the relationship, or possibly the influence, of all events throughout our universe.

Thus, influence, or relationship, is the reason for everything that happens. This, too, renders the statement as "true".

There are those in the New Age cosmology who believe that every single event is intentionally caused by one thing, and one thing alone--human free will. And, from what I have gathered, there is quite a large number of people who believe this theory. And who can say that it is wrong? None of the viewpoints that I have gathered concerning this fascinating phrase provide proof. Each theory stands alone, unproven, with holes in it. But are those holes really there? Or does the lack of evidence represent the limitations of the human mind, when it does not want to understand? To actually acknowledge that souls choose to incarnate into a body that will be born with serious, and painful defects is preposterous to some, and others understand it with an air of factual detachment. Would someone really choose to get cancer? Where did these beliefs originate from? I never said I have all the answers, just more questions as we unravel these mysteries of life.

What does your gut tell you? Perhaps the phrase is correct as it stands, and everything does happen for a reason. But, without being able to specifically identify the "reason" for an event, then the theory cannot hold water. Thus, have some people created an explanation, as in my comments about free will, and it's caught on? At least it's an answer, right?

And there are many who say that every incident or event is a gift, and our self-actualization depends upon our ability to extract the lesson from it. In that case, **karma really is a bitch!**

At its core, everything happens for a reason is a true statement. But, the simplicity of it belies the truth of what the "reason" is. This is where truth can become deception, depending on which of my own, or the myriad of alternate theories, you ascribe to. "The reason" is about relation and interconnectedness. Perhaps we cannot fully comprehend what that means with our dominantly linear thinking patterns. Our intuitive mind must learn to be able to process the complexity of a fully interconnected universe, created by intuitive intelligent design. And there, within that simplicity, is the reason, and the truth.

But let us not forget this popular gem: "$h!t happens".

Chapter 21

Familiarity breeds Contempt

Where did THAT one come from? As if getting to know some-one makes you dislike them? Sure, that can happen, but is that the norm? And is it powerful enough to become a teaching phrase? I don't think it's quite as profound as those who use it believe it to be. But where did it come from?

"Fish and visitors stink in three days" is found within the pages of Benjamin Franklin's *Poor Richard's Almanack*. But those who remem-ber credit somebody else with the coining of this quip--16th century creative writer John Lyly. In his most famous work, *Euphues – the Anatomy of Wit*, Lyly joked that "fish and guests in three days are stale." My question remains whether the title phrase of this section is a twisted version of Lyly's wit, passed down and manipulated from one generation to the next. How has this teaching become so ingrained in our culture? And why?

Like many of the manipulations within this book, words have become tools of control. And words such as these warn us against one, two, or even all three of the following elements, which I call the Three Connections. If **familiarity breeds contempt**, then we believe it best to avoid getting to know others. We also worry that we shouldn't ever let anyone get to know us. And, above all, never ever become too familiar with yourself. What a lonely and meaningless existence! Why, then, are we here?

1. *Getting to know somebody.* **Familiarity breeds contempt** is sometimes meant to temper a new relationship. Think about a budding romantic interest. Oftentimes new or would-be lovers are driven by desire. But sensible friends will encourage these infatuated ones with wisdom to resist and play hard to get. Parents certainly will use this manipulation in order to restrict the amount of time young lovers spend together. But what does this tell us about commitment and long-term relationships? When you really stop to think about it, we are told: "Nobody stays together anymore". It is a lament, and we see divorce rates rising and rampant cohabitation. Should this, then be the norm? My question is: does **familiarity really breed contempt**? Or is this just another lie we are told, which really only serves to sabotage the joy in loving marriages. Why would you want to grow old with someone you dislike? Could this ingrained idiom be serving as yet another self-fulfilling prophecy? It is true only because we believe it to be?

2. *Letting somebody get to know you.* Don't let your guard down. Trust needs to be earned. Think with your head and not with your heart. Aren't those phrases each a part of this symphony of warnings against emotional intimacy? Yet it is most definitely a human yearning--to be known by another. Why then, do we continue to want something that is so bad for us? Or, instead, is the concept of self-isolation indeed harmful to our fragile human psyche? I believe so.

3. *Knowing yourself.* Here's where we come full circle--what goes around comes around. Where do we draw the line? Have I gone too far? But bear with me for a few moments. Socrates and other Greek philosophers are renowned for the discovery that self-awareness is critically important-- "Know thyself". Hundreds of personal development professionals,

life and career coaches, and therapists tout the premise of self-awareness as the first step to any life improvement process. Self-awareness is a journey into self, and an uncovering of all of the questions, discoveries, and synchronicities that go along with such a quest. My facetious question is whether we actually do begin to hold ourselves in contempt as we begin to know ourselves better. And the answer, in many cases, may actually be yes! Oh no! Then it's true!? But wait! I ask you now to look deeper, beneath the surface of who each of us appears to be, and into the fascinating abyss of who we actually are! Maslow's hierarchy of needs is a theory in psychology proposed by Abraham Maslow in his 1943 paper *"A Theory of Human Motivation"*. Self-actualization lies at the top of Maslow's hierarchy. Great philosophers, including Socrates, encourage us to lift the veils between our physical selves and our spiritual selves.

Is there something there, within our souls, within the essence of our true selves? And is this something that is infinitely worthy of love and adoration--from our friends and family as well as from within? Thus, the odyssey of familiarity with self then reveals to us the truth of why we exist. Some philosophers say that mystical experiences are real, and that we experience them because a part of our unconscious is seeking to comprehend our purposes, our true souls, and God. The deeper we go into who we are, the closer we get to this gnosis, which may very well be our truth in pure form.

Some say true love, and twin flame unions lead us to know and understand ourselves better. The partners we choose serve to be reflections of what we have not yet discovered about ourselves. Relationships in conflict are said to be mirrors of our own shadow material. These theories take us all the way into soul discovery--our own and those of others. As mentioned, discovery of our soul, remembrance of our purpose, and connection to a divine creator are all elements toward enlightenment. Learning what it truly means to be human is liberating and joyful. Separation is painful, and unnatural. "**Familiarity breeds contempt**" goes against all of my sensibilities, as the underlying message is isolationism. Upon examination, this lie can be categorized as evil. What else, then, are we missing?

What greater irony exists than satire turned into a weapon? Humans have a propensity, whether it is intentional or not, to seize upon a concept and mindlessly make it viral. In the age of fake news and internet sharing, I wonder: will this corrupt practice worsen, and continue its destructive course? Will harmful missives continue to negatively impact an entire world, for generations?

So, I have taken a silly little euphemism and turned it into a sinister and nefarious deceit, haven't I? Some ask me: "Where do you come up with this stuff"? **You don't want to know.**

Chapter 22

It's the Thought That Counts

Oh, so now we get credit just for *thinking* about doing something nice? I jest, but please note how easy it is to use that excuse when we have fallen down on the job. When we let ourselves off the hook by saying **it's the thought that counts**, we quite possibly validate an error. And within the ensuing rant, you will learn about one of my pet peeves--misguided gifts or help, from one to another.

Consider the "thought". Thinking is a function of the brain. Activity within the brain is nothing short of miraculous--from our automatic responses (breathing, heartbeat, etc.) to the multidimensional superconsciousness that can be activated there. But within our earthbound, very human mind is something called the ego. We've all heard of it. According to Dr. Leopold Bellak (1916–2000), some of the twelve main responsibilities of the ego include judgment, reality testing, impulse control, and defensive functioning--all good things. But, now consider the word ego as we associate it with behaviors such as arrogance, pride or narcissism--now we have entered the realm of not-so-good things. Because now the thinker believes that his or her thoughts are so valuable to another, no action is required. And what exactly are these thoughts that count? They may indeed be good thoughts, but what is the benefit of such to the receiver? Is it tangible?

Is it helpful? Does it demonstrate love? Or did it, indeed, miss the mark? But don't worry, there's always a good excuse: "My ego did it"!

Let us talk about those who decide to help others, but *they* decide *how* they want to help, without considering if that particular form of their assistance is truly helpful. I guess the idea is that if you're offering *something*, then that should be good enough? C'mon people. We can do better than that! This has horseshoes and hand grenades written all over it.

Think about times when we carelessly buy a lousy gift for someone, and then expect heaps of gratitude. And, I get that we may say **it's the thought that counts** in order to teach (especially kids) to appreciate. But some children can be pretty good detectors of bunk, and when they receive gifts that are all wrong it's written all over their faces. So, the lie becomes this: those children are expected to pretend that the gift is wonderful, even when it isn't. Therein lie other distortions: insincerity, and unrequited gratitude and appreciation. We tell our children to fib! But I do need to play devil's advocate for a moment here. I concede that there are people who make great efforts to choose gifts, or to offer help, but they miss the mark through no fault of their own. These honest efforts most certainly deserve recognition, and in this case, we acknowledge the thought, and it really does count.

Before we move on, though, I do have another point about teaching children (and, yes, some adults) about appreciation and gratitude. My viewpoints may seem odd but hear me out. Gratitude is considered a coherent emotion. It is uplifting and can create a good vibe that is almost visceral at times. People who are feeling grateful or appreciative most often wear it right out front--their eyes light up, they smile, they feel an impulse to hug, and so on. Appreciation and gratitude are *feelings*. They are not things that we give back. Helping another or giving a gift should be done in the spirit of love and generosity which results in something good for someone else. That "something good" should include the wonderful feeling of gratitude that person may experience. It is for them and not for you. If a giver is expecting something in return, then what we have is now a transaction, and it is a conditional one as well. I give, so that I will receive. What if, instead, we extracted our gratitude from understanding and appreciating that we were *able* to offer a gift, or assistance, or good feelings to someone else? Can we educe our gratitude from within? Can one extend appreciation to oneself? Give it a try. We now can give without condition and feel gratitude that we have the means to do so. None of that is dependent upon anybody else. It doesn't matter if the person you are helping expresses or even experiences gratitude. Self-satisfaction and reward are all within the power of the giver--no expectations and no conditions are placed upon the recipient. That may truly be a thought that counts.

The good news is, they do exist--people who would never use the phrase **it's the thought that counts**. I have a good friend who really gets it. When one of us asks for help, the other shows up and asks, "What do you need?" This is loving help, given without limitations, without ego, and with no expectation. It is our pledge to each other. And, regardless of what we deem to be "what she really needs", we hold our tongues. A good friend offers herself, or himself, first. Can you give in that manner? It isn't always easy, especially when you truly believe that you know better than they do. Putting personal convictions aside is often quite a challenge and allowing people freedom to choose is not always easy. So let us, instead, look upon one another with understanding—that, my friends, is a wonderful gift.

I return now to my original complaint. When we use the phrase **it's the thought that counts,** we are indeed trying to cover something up--or at least most of the time we are. What if we were completely honest: "Yes, I got stuck with the booby prize from the office swap party, and I re-gifted it to you. But it's the thought that counts"? This sounds silly, but really--if we shouldn't say it, then think about, perhaps, not doing it. So now we have uncovered another deception: re-gifting! But this really isn't news to anyone, is it? Let us continue in the direction of honesty. When we drop the ball for somebody, we dropped the ball. Instead of trying to whitewash it with a manipulation, a more appropriate response could be to say, "I'm sorry". Then we pick up the ball, have a do-over, look to the heavens and wonder if it maybe it *is* better to give than to receive!

PART 6

HUMANITY

The study of lies is a study of paradox. There are many examples of how we say one thing, yet we live another. Our words can serve to belie ourselves. As do our "tells".

Let us talk about accountability--this concept is touted all over the place. At home, school, and in business, leaders everywhere strive to hold people accountable for their actions and behaviors. And, we are expected to hold ourselves accountable. Still, we continue to carelessly toss around a whole bunch of disempowering lies, such as:

Life isn't fair. I find this phrase to be brutally disempowering.

That's the way the cookie crumbles. This, too, is mentioned elsewhere within this book, and more than once! It is a companion phrase with other lies that indicate we have zero control over our own lives. Bunk!

It could be worse. Wow, how I hate that one! Ask anyone who knows me. My blood boils when this phrase is carelessly thrown out there. The statement is not exactly a lie, rather it is an insensitive, nonchalant way for someone to say they don't give a $h!t! Really!

And you know what I'm talking about. When someone has a plight, or a mishap and hears another say it could be worse, perhaps it takes the severity out of the situation. But watch how you use that one. I have heard it used in devastating situations, and during extremely unacceptable circumstances. It can often be an attempt to get off the hook, or an excuse to behave badly. Believe you me, I've seen it in action! Next time you feel tempted to drop that one, think first. You may, instead, choose to have a little empathy.

Do as I say, not as I do. Of course, this reliable lie has become a joke (sort of), but I had to throw it in there for old time's sake. My understanding of this is similar as to the description of the Telephone game (In the Introduction to this book). It humorously demonstrates what happens, every day. We use this phrase when we know we are behaving badly, but we don't want anyone else to act up. See how this connects with the gem mentioned in the introduction for the Relationships section: practice what you preach.

In 1987, *House of Games* was released. This interesting movie is all about deceit, intrigue, and tells. Lindsay Crouse plays the role of Dr. Margaret Ford, a savvy psychiatrist with enough attitude to make her dangerous. In an encounter with Joe Mantegna, starring as "Mike", Margaret sees him for the bully he is, and calls him off in defense of one of her patients. Now satisfied that she is in control of the situation, the good doctor develops a relationship with Mike, who leads her in a fascinating game of cat and mouse. I won't be a spoiler, but once you watch this film it may forever change your perspective on human propensity to cheat, and to lie. You may, indeed say **everyone has their price**!

As humans, our tells ares oftentimes seen within our own body language. Since we are covering entertainment here, there's more. In 2009, Fox network premiered a new series: *Lie to Me**. The cast of characters features a body language expert. Actually, Dr. Cal Lightman is better described as a body language genius. This human lie detector can instantaneously spot even the subtlest of deceptions. It's all about Facial Action Coding, micro expression, body language, and psychology. Imagine Dr. Lightman being your dad? Don't even try to pull one over on this guy.

Moving forward with the connection between lies and the human body, there are continuing mysteries. By now we must acknowledge that some of the deceptions exposed within this book you are reading, are taught, and passed down from generation to generation. They are expressed as truth. These are lies that, for many, have become and continue to be truths. Thus, if one is weaving a tale, what difference does it make whether it is true or not? If someone asserts a thing as fact, even if it isn't, and he or she actually believes it to be so, then is that person is lying? Is deceptive body language present, and is a tell detectable, when believed lies are entraining us?

Just a teeny bit more with the body language (although loosely connected). The odd phrase "**fake it 'til you make it**" has become immensely popular. Yet within this well-meaning (aren't they all) mantra, we see another illusion. If you are faking it, then are you lying? If you're unable to do something, yet you can fool everyone by "faking it", then perhaps you're not really faking at all? Just sayin'. See how far this has gone? We are told to lie to ourselves, tell ourselves we aren't good enough, and therefore we decide to deceive everyone else. I know, I know, it's a confidence thing and I'm looking at it all wrong. But, here's an idea: let's all just say: "You've got this!"

Further, as mentioned in the Introduction pages of this book, how do the lies that we believe construct the limiting beliefs that we hold? And what, if any, possible impact does a lie have on our physicality? Could there be a part of us, deep within our subconscious, that recognizes truth from untruth? And does this realization have an impact, somewhere in our cellular structure? Many theories indicate that cellular memory is real. Some believe that memories are imprinted on DNA and physically passed to the next, or a future generation. How far does this go, and are lies worse than we can even know?

I would be remiss, especially in this section, if I did not broach the subject of propaganda. In a rare moment, I will not overthink, or overcomplicate. Instead I will make this statement painfully simple:

Brainwashing is a form of manipulation. Lies are a method of brainwashing. Propaganda is a tool for the effective brainwashing, through lies and manipulations, of an entire population. Brainwashing by those with tendencies to hate leads to war and atrocities. What could be worse?

Chapter 23

We're Only Human

I really hate hearing people say this. To me, this statement is designed to verbally put humans down. Everyone knows what happens when self-esteem erodes. So why, then would we continue to engage in words that are nothing but destructive. This statement, **we're only human**, is a rollup of disempowering downers. These stories we tell range from the lowest information that **we are born sinful**, to ridiculous teachings that "**humans are flawed**", and everything in between. Low self-esteem in an individual can lead to devastating circumstances. Imagine now a planet full of people who believe this sane premise. We have an entire population of people who believe they are sinful, worthless, possibly even hopeless. What is wrong with this picture?

These humble opinions of mine are just that, mine. But I'm not so humble when I call b.s. on statements that teach us that we are dirty sinners just because we are born. That doesn't make any sense to me, but it continues to be taught by organized religious groups all over the planet. Catholics are evolving away from this teaching, as they have taken a new approach to the different hells such as limbo and the seven terraces of purgatory. Even growing up Catholic, I could never get my head around these teachings, as I tried to imagine Limbo, and an infinite number of unbaptized infants, having died in a sinful state, floating around separate from everything--from other souls, from love, from God. And these poor, innocent spirits were relegated to Limbo for all of eternity. Did I have that wrong? Surely, I am missing something.

Flaws. Wow. What is that? I don't understand why we criticize each other so heavily. Didn't God say everything He created was good? I've heard so many people tout that God doesn't make mistakes, but then those same people turn around and admit that we're all flawed. What about the other creations? Are leopards flawed, or goats? What about trees and grass? Are they flawed? Why is it just us humans?

And those flaws--really! They can be anything, and everything. But once we learn that we're just doomed sinners, do the other things really even matter? Here's a short list, by category, of what we consider flaws:

Our bodies--beauty standards change like the wind. It's mind boggling how body sculpting trends evolve. And fashion is nearly impossible to keep up with these days. One week it's the thigh gap, and the next day it's butt implants. Really, are we that horrible in our natural state? And now we actually have a movement that teaches us to love our flaws! Can't we stop the nonsense?

Our minds--are we smart enough, dedicated enough, ambitious enough, going places, and have the right career? In addition to all of these societal expectations, we judge each other quite harshly for our political positions. Some among us have even volunteered for the role of thought police.

Consider now an alternate outcome, and don't take this personally. When we constantly reinforce the notion that we're only human, we suddenly have an ace in the hole. Our expectations, based upon this limiting perspective, are, therefore, also limited. This perspective can be leveraged to absolve us of responsibility.

In an attempt to be humble, people really do say some pretty self-deprecating things. Is it arrogant to rebut the entire teaching about humans being somehow less than perfect? Do we retain our humility in doing so, as long as we extend that perception of perfection to every human? Admittedly, that won't always come easy. So, my philosophical question is this: is the acceptance of our humanity as undesirable really done under false pretenses? Do we agree that our humanity is all about sin? Or are we applying this belief to ourselves in order to justify what we think of others? First, we must admit that we, individually, are not flawed and it's all been a big lie. But next, and here's where it gets tricky, we admit that no humans are flawed. This means that we see each other as truly being in God's image--all of us.

What I just described may or may not be an easy task. But let us keep going with this. Upon self-examination, are we really flawed? Do we dare to expect our lives to manifest perfection? What motivates us to keep fighting the good fight? Why can't we be living in a state of gratitude for our divine humanity? These questions represent just how incredibly damaging limiting beliefs, low self-esteem, and lies can be. The intention behind **we're only human** is most definitely fake news.

Chapter 24

What You See is What You Get

This phrase, once again, hammers home the perceived randomness of human life. We are repeatedly told that things are, and should be, beyond our control. Several falsehoods are employed to keep people in a state of acquiescence. This is a big one. Here are a few more, just to hammer *my* point home.

That's that way the cookie crumbles.
Everything happens for a reason.
Don't rock the boat.
Too good to be true.
Leave well enough alone.
Seeing is believing.
Keep your fingers crossed.

Lies! All lies! Disguised as clever little proverbs! And they are all connected to each other--interwoven like a complex web that holds us captive.

The Abraham Hicks teachings give us a fresh viewpoint--quite an opposite approach to life than that of the **"what you see is what you get"** paradigm. In fact, these teachings explain that when we become stuck on something as "the way it is", we cut ourselves off from intending something we desire. Esther Hicks, who is a fantastic speaker and a loving guide, has even been described as a "pointer". She points at what she wants. According to the teachings of this organization, and they have written an abundance of books on the subject, one of the worst things we do is to focus on what's happening around us when it is not influencing us in a positive way. By influencing, Mrs. Hicks defines by describing that many people become stuck in a rut of believing based solely upon observation. We cannot help observing our situations, this much is true. But by becoming emotionally locked in to negative circumstances, the Abraham Hicks theory tells us this activity prevents us from seeing the possibilities and opportunities that are either thinly veiled or, perhaps, right under our noses!

We all have the ability to put this theory into action. Don't let anyone tell you otherwise. There will always be people who will roll their eyes and scoff at practices they do not ascribe to. Good for them. Now my question becomes: what do you see?

In my mind's eye, I see opportunity. I see beauty. I see a home, a vehicle, and loving relationships. Thus, is the direction of my focused intention. Additionally, there are things that I see, which are not physically manifested. But I still see them. And this, friend, is the nugget from the Abraham Hicks work, and from other sources that teach about the law of attraction. In my belief system we get what we see--but the discrepancy lies in what it is that we see, and what we believe.

Our physical eyes may behold situations and conditions which are, at best, less than desirable for us. People may experience an inability to find a job or be entrenched in a profession they do not enjoy. Others may be involved in a romantic relationship that is less than fulfilling, or perhaps even miserable. Or, some may be single and hoping to find a romantic partner. And then there's the issue of finances--the shortage or even the mishandling of money. These circumstances, and others in kind, may very well be what many people "see" every day. And yes, I concede, this is what they "get".

"**What you see is what you get**" becomes a manipulation the moment it is intended to indicate that options are limited by our physical sight only. As I described above, we must learn to see what it is that we want, regardless of what the current manifestations tell us. This is important. At the precise moment when this occurs, we then turn "**seeing is believing**" into "believing is seeing". And then we discover the idioms and catchphrases that truly empower, and do not defeat.

The sky's the limit.
Shoot for the stars.
Dream big.
The world is your oyster.

Dr Wayne Dyer (1940-2015) brought us the concept of intention. His visionary work was certainly ahead of his time. He had tremendous insight into the power of changing focus. Dr. Dyer's 2005 book, *The Power of Intention,* is a must read!

Do you see what I did there? Look back at the previous paragraph--note the vocabulary: intention, visionary, insight, focus, power. These words are uplifting. They describe limitlessness. Use these words, understand the principles behind them, embody them and your life will change.

Ajna is a Sanskrit word that is believed to be associated with perception. This is the name for our Third Eye, our chakra, or energy center that gives us a different dimensional vision. The guru chakra is all about intuition and is found in the area of our brow. This is the eye through which dreams and visions of the past and future are viewed. A healthy state of Anja gives us access to what is real and what is not. Lies are intended to blind us from the truth. Our Third Eye is where we perceive and know. A deep study of the seven chakras, and a conscious and intentional awakening of them, gives us freedom from the burdens that others will place upon us.

When we learn to see through our extra sensory sight, the Ajna, then we can identify what we truly seek through an unlimited scope of options and possibilities. Be a cosmonaut. See, and seek, and see more. Discover what lies hidden in plain sight. Rock that boat!

Chapter 25

The Fall of Man

"And the man said, The woman whom thou gavest to be with me, she gave me of the tree, and I did eat. And the Lord God said unto the woman, What is this that thou hast done? And the woman said, The serpent beguiled me, and I did eat." (Genesis 3:12-13 KJVA).

Does this teaching still hold the same power as it has for thousands of years? Does anybody really believe this anymore? Those in my circle don't. But I need to remember that people I hang around with are like me, that's the nature of socializing. But how many live outside of my little world, and still ascribe to the intentional misinterpretations that unceasingly bombard us.

What really happened that day in Paradise? I assert that the traditional interpretation is perhaps not quite as we have thought. Let us break this concept, **"the fall of man"**, down into smaller bites: fruit, gender, and snakes. These are the critical elements at play here. God has strategically set the chessboard for this game.

Picture the scene: the beautiful and nourishing tree which, supposedly contains divine knowledge and power, is positioned in the center of Eve's breathtakingly pristine and perfect world. The evil serpent is nearby and is a formidable opponent for Eve. She is innocent, childlike, and until now we have not heard her thoughts on this tree and its fruit. From the verses that ensue, we believe that she simply obeyed the command to never touch it. What happens next is open to an infinite collection of interpretations. I defend mine as having the same potential for truth as the others. No sacrilege is intended here--only dialogue.

Fruit. Perhaps Eve was curious. Perhaps, in her innocence, she did not even understand the concept of disobedience. I can only imagine the exquisite perfection of all the herbs, vegetables, and beautiful fruits surrounding Eve as she experienced the Earth's gorgeousness. Everything she could have possibly desired was right there, all around. Yet, God was holding back. He chose a tree, right in the midst of all, and lovely to look at, and imposed limitations. His restrictions were preventing the pair from experiencing wisdom(?). Within that bite of the sacred fruit lay the power of God, Himself, and the knowledge of all that is. In her humanity, which is today often described as dirty, even sinful, Eve ate. But we must understand her error: **she's only human**.

Gender. Imagine a Venn diagram of two intersecting circles. In terms of set theory, the shared, or overlapping area is called the Union. Coincidence? Yes, my way of thinking may appear a little bit.... different, shall we say? Indulge me, please! I see the Union as being the human being. Did you follow? The circles represent a number of things, in pairs. All definitions of the circles, to me, are all about creation and support a number of different viewpoints.

The circles are Earth and God. Earth is the matter, and God is the energy. Humans are an ecosystem, as is the earth that physically supports them. Spirit is breathed into the human, as consciousness.

The circles are the push/pull energy defined as fundamental interactions: magnetic and electric. This is Physics but is connected to esoteric theories where these forces are said to be the forces of the female and male bodies, causing an attraction activity.

The circles are God. Finally, we think "twin flames". Some say God is genderless, some say God is both male and female, as would be depicted by both circles representing God. Men joke about getting in touch with their feminine sides. It's really a thing. But let's come back to Earth now!

Snakes. They've been given a really bad rap. Snakes are pretty interesting creatures. As they grow and develop, they shed their old skin and leave it behind. To someone like me, this is quite symbolic. As spirit animals, the snake makes me think of being grounded--and that's a challenge for me. Snakes mostly travel right on the earth--feeling, sensing, smelling, tasting, learning. This is grounding at its finest. Of all the creatures in the animal kingdom, I see the serpent as the one carrying the secrets of Mother Earth. That, to me, is sacred. Yet we are taught that the snake represents evil. Could it be true?

In other mystery schools, the snake represents Kundalini energy—sexual, powerful, and demonstrative of the sacred feminine consciousness. The ancient practices and beliefs about kundalini and its omniscient creative power became oppressed, as were the people that practiced and understood them. Kundalini Yoga appears to be making a comeback, as humans rediscover the holiness of their bodies. What if I made just a tiny tweak to Alexander Pope's proverb from "An Essay on Criticism"? How about this: to err is just to err, to be human is divine.

And about Medusa....really? Actually depicting a woman, with snakes on her head, who somehow makes men die just because they looked at her? On one hand, I can say there's a lesson for you men out there! But I know it's a myth, and I get really drawn in. But really--can't we more easily associate snakes with something having to do with male humans? Right? Think hard.

Why is the snake demonized? You tell me!

> *Interesting side note: I wrote this piece on the second day of the Wavespell of the Red Serpent--an ancient 13-day energy and synchronicity cycle.*

My conclusion is this: did any of this, allegorically, metaphorically, or whatever, actually happen? Probably not. Then what this story teaching us? Or is this entire perspective serving as the greatest self-fulfilling, self-imposed prophecy of all time? Is this not the ultimate weapon of power--to convince a human that they are separate from God? If God's word has been manipulated into a tool of subjugation, then I can't really imagine anything more destructive to the human psyche.

Now, as this narrative was once written, can it not be rewritten? The author of Genesis channeled revelations from God. Can we not do the same? What if by creating a new perspective, and believing that we are still "good", as He created us to be, we experience a new, self-fulfilling paradigm? Consider this: God planted the sacred tree right in the middle of this perfect world. The snake represents our life force, the fruit is nourishment, and the tree of life is gnosis, enlightenment, and a return to knowing God and His pure, unchanging love.

Chapter 26

Charity Begins at Home

This manipulation, **charity begins at home**, is one that I heard quite often during my childhood, and it always bewildered me. To an unsophisticated child, this phrase appeared to be an escape clause--or a reason why we should not extend any of our precious resources to anyone outside of our household. As an adult, I decided to explore this.

During that process, I realized how badly this phrase has been twisted into a serious manipulation, with an insidious intent. It was difficult to see this phrase in a humorous light, but that truly is the mission of this book. So, with the reminder ringing in my head: it is always darkest before the dawn, I tackled this challenge.

In my first book, *Pray Without Ceasing*, I wrote about the phrase **charity begins at home** in a chapter about Love, and here's why: the words love and charity used to mean the same thing. *Both* words meant love. Or, at least from a biblical perspective they did. Keeping that in mind for now, let us break down the phrase.

Many people believe the teaching of **charity begins at home** is scripture from the Holy Bible. But this statement first appears in Sir Thomas Browne's 1642 book, *Religio Medici*. Below is an excerpt from Browne's book:

"Charity.

But how shall we expect charity towards others, when we are uncharitable to ourselves? Charity begins at home, is the voice of the world; yet is every man his greatest enemy, and, as it were, his own executioner." — Thomas Browne, *Religio Medici*.

This section of *Religio Medici* isn't about charity at all, or at least it isn't about charity in the material distribution sense. My interpretation of this phrase speaks to me of self-love. Charity, in this example, means love. And home is defined as self. What Browne is doing here, is espousing a philosophy, and a common truth, that humans are not very good at loving themselves. Therefore, Browne's conclusion is no secret--one must first love oneself or there is nothing to extend to others. We now enter the interconnected realms of love, self-love, selfishness, and generosity. Humanity is constantly engaged in a battle--we conditionally love others because we conditionally love ourselves; we fear a lack of love, so we refuse to give it; we sacrifice our own sense of self love because of social conditioning; all in the hopes of possessing love in abundance for ourselves and for all. An infinite number of dynamics result from a limitation of charity, regardless of how one chooses to define it.

It is important to now return to the biblical definition of charity, as was earlier mentioned. 1 Corinthians 13 is where Saint Paul speaks quite clearly of charity.

> "Charity suffereth long and is kind; charity envieth not; charity vaunteth not itself, is not puffed up, doth not behave itself unseemly, seeketh not her own, is not easily provoked, thinketh no evil; rejoiceth not in iniquity, but rejoiceth in the truth; beareth all things, believeth all things, hopeth all things, endureth all things." (1 Corinthians 13:4-7 KJVA).

But what happened in the early 1970's? A new translation appeared: The New International Version.

> "Love is patient, love is kind. It does not envy, it does not boast, it is not proud. It does not dishonor others, it is not self-seeking, it is not easily angered, it keeps no record of wrongs. Love does not delight in evil but rejoices with the truth. It always protects, always trusts, always hopes, always perseveres." (1 Corinthians 13:4-7 NIV).

Some say this changes everything. Others say this continues to validate the synonymy between the words love and charity. Some say we have two discrete concepts. And now, to me, we have ambiguity, distortion, and loopholes.

Today's society defines charity as the act of giving material items to others, also defined as "donating". As such, the word charity has inherited a negative connotation. Now, depending upon how you look at it, or which end of the action you find yourself on, the experience is oftentimes less than a positive one. Here's why:

Receiving charity, or just being in a state of need of financial and material support, has become something embarrassing. Perhaps this was always so, but in my lifetime I have seen an increase in arguments about things such as welfare reform, food stamps, SNAP Program, and "Obamacare". I have seen people at doctors' offices humiliated for using public medical assistance. And I have witnessed customers hurling insults at the marketplace when they see someone using food assistance funds to purchase necessities for their family. Sometimes people who are in need of assistance often will not accept the help that may be available to them--they may be fearful of the shame that will likely accompany the much-needed assistance. I, for one, certainly would dread trying to get through the checkout line and having somebody examine my groceries and loudly announce that her tax dollars are paying for my shampoo and bananas. Those whose need is desperate enough will take what is offered, yet they are, by many, considered a drain on society. And usually these people are determined as unworthy.

Giving charity, referred to as alms in days of old, has suddenly become something that happens only when the recipient is determined to be deserving. Thus, it becomes a cyclical issue as those who are poor, or in need, are considered, by many, to be in their current state because they are sinful, lazy, or out of line with God. In other words, the poor or less fortunate are most often undeserving. This definition of "undeserving" may be fabricated to avoid that other long-time saying: '**Give until it hurts**". I wrote about the topic of generosity in the chapter entitled "There's No Such Thing as a Free Lunch". That section is a little more high-spirited. So far, in this chapter, I still haven't been able to find the humor. I'll keep trying.

Charity begins at home is a statement that conjures up visions of greed, hoarding, isolationism, judgement, division, lack of empathy, and a decision not to love. To me, if there is such a thing as sin then this would be it. Which now is reminding me of the tithe. And the voices of some of our country's prominent televangelists are creeping into my head.

Seems to me that tithing meant giving back to God. In earlier times, this would mean choosing the first or best of your income- -crops, livestock, fruit, etc. One tenth of the firstfruits were to be offered as sacrifice. The yield would be ceremonially placed, or burnt, as recognition that God had provided, and will continue to provide. Whether you ascribe to this belief or not, this is the history of it. But today, we are a mechanized, money-based, property owner based, corporate, hierarchical society. For better or for worse, no longer do we ceremonially burn goats, at least not in my neighborhood. Enter the televangelist. What a brilliant opportunity. These charismatic people will be more than happy to manage our tithes for us. Or course! Give your money to them, and God will multiply it and give it back to you in great abundance. So, I ask--is that tithing? Or is that an invest- ment? These two things are very, very different, aren't they? And in no way, shape, or form does this resemble charity.

Now tell me this--what kind of charity occurs at home? When I imagine family members taking care of each other, and parents providing for their children, I certainly don't liken those activities to charity, unless we redefine charity, as it once was, as love. Okay. I get that. We love, first, our own. After all, **blood is thicker than water**, no? Or has this teaching now become a directive to stop caring about others? Is this "us" and "them"? But, by understanding charity according to the modern definition, what kinds of charity, or donations, would we see at home? This doesn't even make sense, especially when we throw in another disclaimer to the repertoire: **God helps those who help themselves.**

At the end of the day, I consider **charity begins at home** to be a heartless disregard for everyone else in the world. What about neighbors helping neighbors? Where is "home"? Does it extend beyond the walls of our house? What about extended family who live elsewhere? Don't they count? Browne's original intent has, perhaps been lost in translation. To me, it makes so much more sense than...wait! Come to think of it, I don't think anyone actually ever explained this to me. Perfect! Then today I begin with a clean slate, and I reverse all harm caused by this teaching, as, to me, nothing good can really come from this.

So, let us love, give, receive, and care for each other. Let us remember that Earth is your home and mine. Remember that we are all of the same race--the human race. And always take care of yourself. Keep your cup full of love and charity!

PART 7

SPIRIT

This is where we look at truth and lies from an expanded perspective. The sections within this book are sequenced, and numbered. To me, this represented a linear progression of ideas, as they evolved through different phases of human lives. The numerology of seven was intentionally coded into this book. And this last section, the seventh, is a call to further self-examination, and then mastery. Here is where we understand that the brain does what the mind tells it to do. The innate brain is where we go now.

What secrets do we keep, tucked away deep into our shadows? We all hold them. The writing of this book was a commitment to the unlocking of my beliefs. The intent was to examine rigid beliefs and statements of finality and convert to a more fluid way of approaching life's ups and downs. But, as the concepts unfolded and turned into words on a page, an uneasiness began to arise. This odd feeling plagued me, and began to intrude into my snarky little ideas, and into my deepest discoveries. I finally figured it out. It was, not surprisingly, a question, and the question was this: what lies are you telling yourself?

As I pondered, I realized that, yes, the most devastating lies are those we tell ourselves. Each of us has a secret chamber, as did Bluebeard. Within us, locked away, crouches the evidence of our own deceptions, and tremendous pain. This is called our shadow material by some. Others refer to it as our underworld. Now, a journey into truth can be as deep and as adventurous as you desire it to be, and can take you to great heights of gnosis, and deep caverns of trepidation. Unraveling lies is not a journey for the faint of heart.

And, how do we know that what we now believe to be truth is actually so? I wrote my remedies for all the lies I have been told, I cited Bible verses, and I created what I thought were logical arguments. But how do any of us really know? Is this like waking up from a dream, only to find that you're still experiencing another dream? Is it human arrogance-- to believe we know and understand? Did the serpent not tantalize Eve with the prospect of being like God?

Now I am compelled to consider that perhaps my children will go on to discover that many things I said to them were not true. With an air of satisfaction, I may announce something as fact, when later they may wonder: "What was Mama thinking?" Will they be angry, and feel betrayed and hurt? Perhaps. Will they then find forgiveness, for me and for everyone who made these mistakes? I pray they do. Thus, as example for them, I do that first.

When does the conditioning kick in for me and for you? Once again, we are visited by that little voice saying, "You know nothing". Further, taking the position of knowing nothing may be the very thing that prepares the way for understanding. This is a circular discussion, a mysterious philosophy, and a question without an answer.

According to my galactic signature, I am the Blue Cosmic Night, with a mantra that is quite fitting for me. Truthfully, it was somewhat of a surprise to discover that my soul description may indeed abide within the oracle: "I endure in order to dream; transcending intuition; I seal the input of abundance with the cosmic tone of presence;

I am guided by the power of accomplishment". The pondering of the mantra felt like a new and deeper discovery of self. However--did I truly discover the ancient words that describe my soul personality? Or did I become an embodiment of that soul because I imprinted the description upon myself? Which, if either, is true? How will I know?

In summary, if, for whatever reason, you skipped right to this page of the book and didn't read anything else I wrote, that's fine. Although you missed out on some eye-rolls, rants, and wacky notions, here's what I want you to know: truth is freedom. Time is freedom. Money is freedom. Your Inner Child represents freedom. Love is freedom, and God is freedom. Find the truth at all costs. Hold tight to it. Make it your rock, your strong tower, and your light that shines in all dark places. Truth is life.

And how remiss would I be if I did not cite here a most well-known and well used bible verse? "and ye shall know the truth, and the truth shall make you free." (John 8:32 KJVA).

Chapter 27

The Lord Gives and the Lord Takes Away

Yes, I am aware that this proverbial statement is in my beloved Holy Bible. But not really. There is much debate among theologians and scholars as to the correct interpretation for this verse from the book of Job. "Naked came I out of my mother's womb, and naked shall I return thither: the Lord gave, and the Lord hath taken away; blessed be the name of the Lord." (Job 1:21 KJVA). My humble opinion is that much of Job is misinterpreted (except, perhaps, the unicorn part) and here's why.

Of all the books in the bible, Job is among the most ambiguous, and the most hotly contested. Ironically, the chapter itself is a series of philosophical debates and dialogues about the true nature of God. The stylized complexity of disagreement within Job, represents two things: the chronicling of a historical event, and a prophecy. Much in the same manner as I described the game of Telephone in the Introduction to this book, we see a scenario, within the book of Job, play out as a recurring, future theme: the ongoing philosophical and dialectal interaction, between humans, regarding the true nature of God. As Job, El´iphaz, Zophar, and Bildad reason, argue, and testify, so, also, do we. When the book comes to a close, Job and his companions part ways, each still contending that his own position is correct. And perhaps each is correct, or perhaps none is correct: not one of these men convinced the others to adopt a different viewpoint. And these same circumstances exist today regarding this important story, and the critical topics which are included. The book of Job, at first glance, is an effort to know and explain God. Yet, after all is said and done, the story is, instead, a snapshot of the nature of humans.

Can we conclude that the entire story of Job, with all of its joys and tragedies, and with all of its real-life drama, is unexplainable by design? If yes, then we must determine that the true nature of God is, likewise, beyond all reason, understanding, and definition.

So then, what is behind the phrase **the Lord gives and the Lord takes away**? Job's declaration, as quoted above, is often defined as relating to life itself--our very existence. Yet a single and nefarious purpose lies within that phrase as spoken today: disempowerment. Now I have wandered into the realm of a particular concept: complete dependence upon God. And here, my friend, please remember there's more than one way to skin a cat.

Like some of the viewpoints expressed within the book of Job, can we imagine God is interacting with us, and micromanaging every moment of our lives? For those who believe this is so, can the lament of Job be reframed? Job's theory is, in fact, restated, and perhaps clarified, in the book of John. "The next day John seeth Jesus coming unto him, and saith, Behold the Lamb of God, which taketh away the sin of the world!" (John 1:29 KJVA). Now we see a benevolent Creator, from whom flows only good things. And one who takes away the bad things.

What does it all mean? That depends upon whether or not you are one who ascribes to the theory that God is, and rightly so, in control--that one must let go and let God. But wait! Where did we first hear that **God helps those who help themselves**?

Could that phrase have been uttered from the same mouths as those who insist that **charity begins at home**? This instruction assists us in creating an excuse and a disclaimer. Has God become a scapegoat in times of loss? Does the phrase **"the Lord gives, and the Lord takes away"** somehow absolve one of responsibility for the outcome of one's life? Or are we, instead, empowered by God, created in His image, equipped to embody purpose, and capable of managing our own lives? Did God tell Job to man up?

More questions--would God really stand by and watch Satan crush such a good and pious man? Does God possibly possess an ego, as humans do? Further, does He, as do we, seek to be considered righteous in the eyes of others? In the final transmission, where God is said to have responded to Job's pleadings, does He explain? Or, once again, have humans projected their own theories of behavior onto God? You decide.

As for the restoration--do the new children, and the new livestock, and the restored life really serve as compensation for the suffering of Job and his early family? After the tragic and agonizing events, does the new cycle of God's giving erase the pain of what was lost? Again, this is for each of us to discern.

By basing this entire chapter on a brief, and certainly inadequate analysis of the book of Job, I understand that I have put all my eggs into one basket. But, in conclusion, even after the realization that man cannot comprehend the mind of God, mankind continues to explain (or should I say "mansplain") God. Have we learned nothing from Job? Or have the teachings within the holy book played out precisely as does a game of Telephone? What did the first player actually say? Does anyone really know? Can we, or will we, ever know?

Chapter 28

Karma's a Bitch

Three times you heard it said now (five if you count the table of contents and the chapter title above) --another deceptive, self-fulfilling condition of the soul. We believe, therefor we create. We say it, and our brain hears and believes. We ask, and we receive. We focus, and we manifest. We dream into existence. **Perception is reality**.

For better or for worse, these are the concepts that shape our humanity. But I introduce the idea of karma because it holds power. The karma itself is not what holds the power. The belief that karma exists is what has a hold on us. This belief can have a profound, and unconscious, impact on the way we think, speak, and behave. Further, karma is defined in dramatically different ways, depending upon each person's association with it, and how the various religions of the world approach it. The word, karma, itself holds a particular vibration and a certain emotion, different for each.

As a child, I was raised in the Roman Catholic faith and spent years of religious education--not studying our holy book, The Bible, but instead being programmed with all of the dogma, the rules, the ritual, and the expectations about what it means to be a good Catholic. To me, even as a grade school child, the missing piece was this: who am I?

What I did learn, was that God loves me. But that he is also jealous, sometimes angry, and always ready to punish. This was terrifying. And I learned that we each were created, by God, to love Him. That was the sole reason for our existence. None of this made sense to me. When I fell off my bike, or something seemingly minor went wrong it was because I was bad, and God was punishing me. Not a good way to live. All I knew was this: the immense, omnipotent, and mysterious power was there, always--seeing every intimate moment of my life, examining even my every thought, waiting for me to mess up. And I did not disappoint!

Even to this day, if I stub my toe, I hear the words "God punished you" ring in my head, I catch my breath, my heart pounds, and I think about what questionable acts I had recently committed. I still ask myself: "Is it true?" That, my friend, is manipulation, it is control, it is programming at its finest. And this theory certainly does not represent the God I now know--the One who created me in loving energy, in His perfect image, in His likeness, and called me "good". In overcoming the toxic teachings about God, and ourselves, have we therefore remediated karma? Or, perhaps it was never there to begin with. This question may very well remain unanswered until after generations of examination, along with evidence. Clarity is still quite elusive for this topic.

My question is now: are we less likely to make mistakes when we live with a loving supportive, benevolent God? Or are we, instead, only able to understand how to be good through fear? Modern parenting styles are trending away from fear and physical punishment-based systems. Teachers are trying to ignore inappropriate behaviors and recognize positive behaviors. And some parents continue to mimic the styles of their own parents. They sometimes realize mistakes were made, but, since that's the way it was, then so shall it be now. Could that be the karma that we continue? It certainly would now define karma as cycles of social patterns that humanity willingly and intentionally repeat, just because. Thus, karma is less an esoteric notion, rather it is a very human behavior pattern, controlled by each of us. Karma is not random, we do not live a less than ideal life because we are being punished for misdeeds in a previous lifetime, and we do not live under the ever-watchful eye of God--waiting to pounce and strike us with that ever-threatening lightning bolt. It is just us humans behaving badly and blaming it on something else. Karma is a lie.

Finally, I introduce another personal philosophy: the concept of service as opposed to obedience. In our attempts to approximate God, we place parental attributes upon Him.** Obedience is a word that indicates authority and submission. It is not my intention to offend those who believe in total submission and compete deference to God for the course of their lives. I respect this pattern as correct and honorable. But I consider my own life to be, instead, one of service to humanity, of my choosing according to soul purpose, and empowered by my Creator. And there are many who do not believe that we have a mystical energy at all, and we are purely biological. Those people are driven by their own moral compass and traditional ethics--this is also a theory and lifestyle deserving of respect because it is right for those who so choose it. In dedicating to service to God, one chooses to draw upon the higher dimensional energies in order to accomplish that for which God has placed a desire within the heart. One serves God, by serving humanity, in a manner which fulfills and satisfies the soul. There is no karma. Low frequency emotions such as fear, hate, and anger are challenges indeed, but are to be transmuted. Love is both the fire and the fuel.

I've waxed philosophical again, but the bottom line is that I do not believe in karma. I don't think we return to Earth and live miserable lives to atone for misdeeds in previous ones. I just don't. Our lives belong to us, given to us by our Creator. We're behind the wheel, we

---

** I refer to God, always, as "Him" (and other masculine pronouns) for the sake of continuity and simplicity. To me, God cannot be defined as having gender. Interesting personal story: one of my children, since the very young age of four of five, spontaneously began to refer to God as "Her" (and consistently feminine pronouns). I welcomed and respected whatever insight was inspiring this idea for her, but you can only imagine the eruption among the old-timers in the family!

choose the roads we take, we make our beds, and we lie in them. I don't see God as taking control of my life, rather as being a source that empowers me to live my soul's purpose. Karma does not come between me and my God.

Still With Me?--Conclusion

Before I close, I wish to mention Michel de Montaigne (1533-1592). This book you are holding is my second, and certainly will not be my last, where each idea is written in similar form to an essay. Montaigne's vast literary contributions include the formal development of the essay, which has endured as a distinct literary style. Aside from that, Montaine was a scholar, an educator, a Humanist, and much more. My admiration for Michel de Montaigne's work deserved explicit expression.

My first book, *Pray Without Ceasing*, contains 24 empowerment topics, with a chapter full of strategies and resources for each. While assembling this work, I was compelled to revisit, and pull some thoughts from the following chapters from that book: Prosperity, Words, Love, and Generosity. Thus, I discovered that these four areas, or very human parts of us, are powerfully impacted by lies and deceptions which are foisted upon us since early childhood. By believing the negative manipulations, we become somewhat limited in our abilities to fully embody, and enjoy, the attributes suggested. Thus, perhaps "limiting beliefs" is a thing. Thus, lies are just errors.

At the onset of the writing, I may have come off as angry, paranoid, and as one ascribing to conspiracy theories. And perhaps I was. You, my dearest reader, have witnessed my struggle, as my style changed from cynical, to bitter, to amused, and to intellectual, depending upon the subject. My mind and emotions were impacted in different ways by the different lies which I sought to investigate. Such is the human condition when experiencing confusion over clarity. Such was my journey--one from low vibrational emotions, such as resentment and anxiety, into higher states of acceptance, understanding, and joy.

Now I am released by my own self-healing and hope to show that discovery to others. Together, my friends, we have travelled through the realization that lies are harmful, dangerous, and even deadly. Recall, now, my ramblings on the power of our words: the very key to life and death is in the power of what we say. When we speak something, especially aloud, our brain hears and believes. Our brain is programmed by our minds, it is designed to serve us, and it does not correct us. We must retrain and reprogram ourselves, our brains, and our psyches. Once awake to the deceptions all around us, and only then, we can begin to heal.

And sometimes I do think we make too much out of limiting beliefs. As mentioned earlier, it is a philosophical argument with a life of its own. Once we *realize* that we are programmed, then that's the battle nearly won. Through the awareness, we shine a light on all of it--a healing and loving warm light. The darkness is gone, the wounds begin to heal, and love comes in. Tom Kenyon, an author, brain research scientist, and psychotherapist, offers channeled messages and incredible insights on his website (see Bibliography). Perhaps we should join the more enlightened among us, including Mr. Kenyon and the higher beings, as they suggest that this is all "one big cosmic joke"?

The Thank Yous!

This was such a fun project! I spoke to many people about my ideas, and I was delighted to hear so many viewpoints. The casual conversations with friends, family, co-workers, and strangers on the street were all critical in this collection of rants. Everyone had an opinion, and everyone was happy to share it with me. This was invaluable as I sorted out the things I wanted to say. After all, you know what they say about opinions!

And I want to acknowledge, with great appreciation, my better half, Walter. He is the quintessential Devil's Advocate and kept me on my toes about each of the "lies" I decided to include in this book. The bantering, bickering, and general badinage were a powerful driving force for me. For that I wish to say a very sincere "thank you"!

Bibliography and Suggested Reading

Arguelles, Jose, *The 260 Postulates of the Dynamics of Time*

Arguelles, Jose, and South, Stephanie. *The Book of the Throne.*

Baum, L. Frank. *The Wonderful Wizard of Oz.* Chicago: George M. Hill Company, 1900

Bellak, Leopold. *Ego Function Assessment, C.P.S.*, Incorporated, 1989.

Berne, Eric. *Games People Play: The Psychology of Human Relationships. UK:* Penguin Life, 2016.

Browne, Thomas, Sir, 1605-1682. *Sir Thomas Browne's Religio Medici, Urn Burial, Christian Morals, and Other Essays.* London:W. Scott, 1886.

Collodi, C. *The Adventures of Pinocchio.* New York: Groset and Dunlap, 1946.

Currie, Robin P., *Pray Without Ceasing, Essays and Godwinks*, Archway Publishing, 2018.

Dyer, Dr. Wayne W. *The Power of Intention: Learning to Co-create Your world Your Way.* Sydney, Australia: Accessible Pub., 2008.

Einstein, Albert. *Ideas and Opinions.* Random House, LLC., 1995.

Fitzgerald, F. Scott. *Babylon Revisited and Other Stories.* New York: Scribner, 2003.

Frankl, Viktor. *Man's Search for Meaning,* 1959 (originally entitled *From Death-Camp to Existentialism).*

Golding, William. *Lord of the Flies.* New York: Holt, Rinehart and Winston.

Harris, Dr. Thomas A. *I'm OK, You're OK.* HarperCollins, 1969.

Hicks, Esther, and Jerry Hicks. *Ask and It Is Given: Learning to Manifest Your Desires.* New Delhi, India: Hay House Publications (India) Pvt., 2017.

Homer. *The Iliad.* Venetus A = Venetus Marc. 822 from the 10th century, 700s B.C.

Kenyon, Tom. *The Hathor Material.*

Kenyon, Tom, and Virginia Essene. *The Hathor Material: Messages from an Ascended Civilisation.* CA 95051: Spiritual Education Endeavors Publishing, 1996.

King, Stephen. *Misery: A Novel.* New York, NY: Pocket Books, 2017.

Lyly, John (1553-1606). *Euphues: The Anatomy of Wit.* 1578.

Maslow, Abraham. *"A Theory of Human Motivation".* 1943

Menglong, Feng (1574-1646), *Stories to Awaken the World,* 1627.

Newton, Michael. *Journey of Souls: Case Studies of Life between Lives.* Woodbury, MN: Llewellyn Publications, 1994.

Orwell, George. *1984.*

Pope, Alexander (1688-1744). *"An Essay on Criticism."*

Perrault, Charles, and Frédéric De. Scitivaux. *Histoires, Ou, Contes Du Temps Passé: Contes.* Paris: Larousse, 2014.

Ra, Kaia. *The Sophia Code.* Kaia Ra and Ra-El Publishing. 2016.

Selig, Paul. *The Book of Truth: A Channeled Text.* New York: TarcherPerigee, 2017.

Skow, Bradford. *Objective Becoming.* Oxford: Oxford University Press, 2016.

Vyasa. *The Bhagavad Gita*, 4th to 5th Century B.C.

Weldon, Sir Anthony, Scott, Walter, and John Francis Rotton. *Secret History of the Court of James the First: Containing, I. Osbornes Traditional Memoirs. II. Sir Anthony Weldons Court and Character of King James. III. Aulicus Coquinariae. IV. Sir Edward Peytons Divine Catastrophe of the House of Stuarts: With Notes and Introductory Remarks: In Two Volumes.* Edinburgh: Printed by James Ballantyne and for John Ballantyne and, Edinburgh, and Longman, Hurst, Rees, Orme, and Brown, London, 1811.

Films:

In Time. Directed by Andrew Niccol. 2011.

The Matrix. Directed by The Wachowskis. 1999.

Star Wars. Created by George Lucas. 1977

Sunshine Cleaning. Directed by Christine Jeffs. 2008.

Willie Wonka and the Chocolate Factory. Directed by Mel Stuart. 1971.

The Devil's Advocate. Directed by Taylor Hackford. 1997.

House of Games. Directed by David Mamet. 1987.

Invasion of the Body Snatchers. Directed by Philip Kaufman. 1978.

Websites:

Tortuga 13:20 https://tortuga1320.com/

Foundation for the Law of Time https://lawoftime.org/

Tom Kenyon https://tomkenyon.com/

Nag Hammad Library http://gnosis.org/naghamm/nhl.html

Center for Disease Control and Prevention https://www.cdc.gov/nchs/fastats/emergency-department.htm

Calendar Referendum Initiative https://13months28days.info/

Musical references:

"Won't get Fooled Again", by Pete Townshend. 1971.

"Imagine", by John Lennon and Yoko Ono. 1975.

"High Hopes", by Jimmy Van Heusen and Sammy Cahn. 1959.

"Life Sucks... And Then You Die!", by Cerebral Fix. 1988.

"Money Changes Everything", by Cyndi Lauper. 1984.

"All You Need is Love", by The Beatles. 1967.

"The Ties That Bind", by Bruce Springsteen. 1980.

"Love is a Battlefield", by Pat Benatar. 1983.

CPSIA information can be obtained
at www.ICGtesting.com
Printed in the USA
LVHW091917090919
630428LV00007B/159/P